THE RECONSTRUCTION OF GEORGIA

STUDIES IN HISTORY, ECONOMICS AND PUBLIC LAW

EDITED BY THE FACULTY OF POLITICAL SCIENCE OF
COLUMBIA UNIVERSITY

VOLUME XIII]   [NUMBER 3

THE

RECONSTRUCTION OF GEORGIA

BY

EDWIN C. WOOLLEY

AMS PRESS
NEW YORK

COLUMBIA UNIVERSITY
STUDIES IN THE
SOCIAL SCIENCES

36

The series was formerly known as
Studies in History, Economics and Public Law.

Reprinted with the permission of Columbia University Press
From the edition of 1901, New York
First AMS EDITION published 1970
Manufactured in the United States of America

Library of Congress Catalog Card Number: 74-120211
International Standard Book Number:
    Complete Set: 0-404-51000-0
    Number 36: 0-404-51036-1

AMS PRESS, INC.
New York, N.Y. 10003

TABLE OF CONTENTS

CHAPTER VIII

CHAPTER IX

CHAPTER X

LIST OF ABBREVIATIONS

A. A. C. = American Annual Cyclopaedia.

B. A. = Address of Bullock to the people of Georgia, a pamphlet dated 1872.

B. L. = Letter from Bullock to the chairman of the Ku Klux Committee, published in Atlanta in 1871.

C. G. = Congressional Globe.

C. R. = Report of the State Comptroller.

E. D. = United States Executive Documents.

E. M. = Executive Minutes (of Georgia).

G. O. D. S. = General Orders issued in the Department of the South.

G. O. H. = General Orders issued from the headquarters of the army.

G. O. M. D. G. = General Orders issued in the Military District of Georgia.

G. O. T. M. D. = General Orders issued in the Third Military District.

H. J. = Journal of the Georgia House of Representatives.

H. M. D. = United States House Miscellaneous Documents.

J. C., 1865 = Journal of the Georgia Constitutional Convention of 1865.

J. C., 1867-8 = Journal of the Georgia Constitutional Convention of 1867-8.

K. K. R. = Ku Klux Report (Report of the Joint Committee of Congress on the Conditions in the Late Insurrectionary States, submitted at the 2d session of the 42d Congress, 1872).

M. C. U. = Milledgeville *Confederate Union.*

M. F. U. = Milledgeville *Federal Union.*

R. C. = Reports of Committees of the United States House of Representatives.

R. S. W. = Report of the Secretary of War.

S. D. = United States Senate Documents.

S. J. = Journal of the Georgia Senate.

S. L. = Session Laws of Georgia.

S. R. = United States Senate Reports.

S. O. M. D. G. = Special Orders issued in the Military District of Georgia.

S. O. T. M. D. = Special Orders issued in the Third Military District.

U. S. L. = United States Statutes at Large.

CHAPTER I

PRESIDENTIAL RECONSTRUCTION

THE question, what political disposition should be made of the Confederate States after the destruction of their military power, began to be prominent in public discussion in December, 1863. It was then that President Lincoln announced his policy upon the subject, which was to restore each state to its former position in the Union as soon as one-tenth of its population had taken the oath of allegiance prescribed in his amnesty proclamation and had organized a state government pledged to abolish slavery. This policy Lincoln applied to those states which were subdued by the federal forces during his administration, viz., Tennessee, Arkansas and Louisiana. When the remaining states of the Confederacy surrendered in 1865, President Johnson applied the same policy, with some modifications, to each of them (except Virginia, where he simply recognized the Pierpont government).

Before this policy was put into operation, however, an effort was made by some of the leaders of the Confederacy to secure the restoration of those states to the Union without the reconstruction and the pledge required by the President. After the surrender of Lee's army (April 9, 1865), General J. E. Johnston, acting under the authority of Jefferson Davis and with the advice of Breckenridge, the Confederate Secretary of War, and Reagan, the Confederate Postmaster General, proposed to General Sherman the surrender of all the Confederate armies then in existence on certain condi-

tions.   Among these was the condition that the executive of
the United States should recognize the lately hostile state
governments upon the renewal by their officers of their oath
of allegiance to the federal Constitution, and that the people of the states so recognized should be guaranteed, so far
as this lay in the power of the executive, their political
rights as defined by the federal Constitution.   Sherman
signed a convention with Johnston agreeing to these terms,
on April 18.   That he intended by the agreement to com-
mit the federal government to any permanent policy is
doubtful.   But when the convention was communicated for
ratification to his superiors at headquarters, they showed the
most decided opposition to granting the terms proposed
even temporarily.   The convention was emphatically dis-
avowed, and on April 26 Sherman had to content himself
with the surrender of Johnston's army only, agreed to on
purely military terms.[1]

Georgia formed a part of the district under the command
of General Johnston.   As soon, therefore, as the news of the
surrender could reach that state, hostilities there ceased.
On May 3, Governor Brown issued a summons for a meeting
of the state legislature to take place on May 22, in order
that measures might be taken "to prevent anarchy, restore
and preserve order, and save what [could be saved] of liberty and civilization."[2]   At a time of general consternation,
when military operations had displaced local government
and closed the courts in many places, when the whole population was in want[3] through the devastation of the war or
through the collapse of the Confederate currency which

---

[1] Alex. Stephens, *The War Between the States,* vol. ii, p. 623; W. T. Sherman,
Memoirs, vol. ii, pp. 346–362.

[2] M. C. U., May 9, 1865.

[3] See the account of the gigantic relief operations of the federal army, A. A. C.,
1865, p. 392.

followed the collapse of the Confederate army,[1] the need of such measures was apparent.

The calling of the legislature incurred the disapproval of the federal authorities for two reasons. First, they regarded it as an attempt to prepare for further hostilities, and they accordingly arrested Brown, carried him to Washington, and put him in prison.[2] Second, in any case, as the disavowal of the convention of April 18 had shown, they did not intend to allow the state governments of the South to resume their regular activities at once, and accordingly the commander of the Department of the South issued orders on May 15, declaring void the proclamation of Joseph E. Brown, "styling himself Governor of Georgia," and forbidding obedience thereto.[3]

The federal army now took control of the entire state government. Detachments were stationed in all the principal towns and county seats, and the commanders sometimes removed the civil officers and appointed others, sometimes allowed them to remain, subject to their direction. Military orders were issued regarding a wide range of civil affairs, such as school administration, sanitary provisions, the regulation of trade, the fixing of prices at which commodities should be sold, etc.[4] The provost marshal's courts were fur-

[1] M. C. U., May 9, 1865.

[2] Letter from Joseph E. Brown to Andrew Johnson, dated May 20, 1865, in the Department of War, Washington. Brown was arrested on May 10. On May 8, upon surrendering the state troops to the federal general Wilson, he had been paroled. (The parole paper is in the above mentioned archives.) Hence the arrest was a violation of his parole. When Wilson entered into the parole engagement he had not been informed how his superiors would regard the summoning of the legislature. Immediately afterward he probably received orders from the central authorities to arrest Brown. He preferred obeying orders to observing his engagement.

[3] G. O. D. S., 1865, no. 63.

[4] See G. O. D. S., 1865, *passim*. Also Savannah *Republican*, May 1, 2, 3, etc. 1865.

ther useful, to some extent, as substitutes for the state courts, whose operations were largely interrupted.[1] Directions to the officers of the Department admonished them that " the military authority should sustain, not assume the functions of, civil authority," except when the latter course was necessary to preserve the peace.[2] This admonition from headquarters, issued after the President's plan for reinstating Georgia in the Union had been put into operation, reflects his desire for a quick restoration of normal government.

President Johnson announced his policy toward the seceded states in his proclamation of May 29, 1865, regarding North Carolina. By it a provisional governor was appointed for that state, with the duty of making the necessary arrangements for the meeting of a consitutional convention, to be composed of and elected by men who had taken the oath of allegiance prescribed by the President's amnesty proclamation of the same date, and who were qualified voters according to the laws of the state in force before the war. The proclamation did not state what the President would require of the conventton, but we may mention by way of anticipation that his requirements were the revocation of the ordinance of secession, the construction of a new state government in place of the rebel government, the repudiation of the rebel debt, and the abolition of slavery within the state. The provisional governor was further authorized to do whatever was " necessary and proper to enable [the] loyal people of the state of North Carolina to restore said state to its constitutional relations to the federal government." [3]

[1] Savannah *Republican*, July 4, 1865. See also James Johnson's proclamation of July 13, 1865, M. F. U. of same date.

[2] M. F. U., July 25, 1865.

[3] U. S. L., vol. 13, 760. The provisional governorship, it may be remarked,

For each of the states subdued in 1865, except Virginia, a provisional governor was appointed by a similar proclamation. On June 17, James Johnson, a citizen of Georgia, was appointed to the position in that state.[1] On July 13th, he issued a proclamation providing for the election of the convention. Delegates were distributed on the basis of the legislature of 1860; the first Wednesday in October was set for the election, and the fourth Wednesday in the same month for the meeting of the convention.[2] Next, the provisional governor undertook the task of securing popular support to the programme of restoration. To encourage subscription to the amnesty oath (a prerequisite to voting for delegates to the convention) he removed the disagreeable necessity of taking it before the military authorities by directing the ordinary and the clerk of the Superior Court of each county to administer it,[3] He made many speeches throughout the state urging the citizens to take the amnesty oath, to enter earnestly into the election of the convention, and to submit quietly to the conditions imposed by the President.

His efforts were very successful. This was partly due to the place he held in public estimation. He was a lawyer widely known and universally respected. It was also partly due to the attitude of Governor Brown. Brown, after a confinement of several weeks in prison at Washington, secured an interview with President Johnson, and satisfied the President that his object in calling the legislature was simply public relief, that he had no intention to prolong the war, but

was characterized by the Secretary of War as "ancillary to the withdrawal of military force, the disbandment of armies, and the reduction of military expenditure by provisional [civil organizations] to take the place of armed force." The salaries of the provisional governors were paid from the army contingencies fund. See S. D., 39th Congress, 1st session, no. 26.

[1] U. S. L., vol. 13, p. 764.

[2] M. F. U., July 13, 1865; A. A. C., 1865, p. 394.

[3] M. F. U., August 15, 1865; A. A. C., *loc. cit.*

calmly submitted to the fact that his side was defeated.[1] This explanation and the spirit displayed were so satisfactory to Johnson that Brown was released, and permitted to return to Georgia. His return, remarked Johnson, " can be turned to good account. He will at once go to work and do all he can in restoring the state." [2] This prediction proved correct. The war governor of Georgia became the type of those Secessionists who practised and counseled quiet acceptance of the terms imposed by the conqueror, as the most sensible and advantageous course. On June 29th he issued an address to the people of Georgia, resigning the governorship, and advising acquiescence in the abolition of slavery and active participation in the reorganization of the state government according to the President's wishes.[3] The assumption of this attitude by Brown grieved and offended some of his fellow Secessionists. But the majority shared his opinion. The provisional governor was welcomed, and and his speeches approved on all sides.[4] The result was that the convention which met on October 25th was a body distinguished for the reputation and ability of its members.

The convention was called to order by the provisional governor, and chose as permanent chairman Herschel V. Johnson.[5] Then a message from the provisional governor was read, suggesting certain measures of finance and other state business requiring immediate action, suggesting also certain alterations in the state judiciary, but especially pointing out the chief objects of the convention, viz., the passage of those acts requisite for the restoration of the

[1] Letter from Brown to Johnson, dated May 20, 1865, archives of the Department of War, Washington.

[2] Letter from Johnson to Stanton dated June 3, 1865, in same archives.

[3] M. F. U., July 11, 1865.

[4] M. F. U., July 18.   Savannah *Republican*, July 1 and 3.

[5] J. C., 1865, p. 3.

state.[1]   These measures the convention quickly proceeded to pass.   On October 26th it repealed the ordinance of secession and the ordinance ratifying the Confederate constitution.;[2] by paragraph 20 of article I. of the new constitution it abolished slavery in the state; and on November 8th, the last day of the session, it declared the state debt contracted to aid the Confederacy void.[3] The convention provided for a general state election on the following November 15th, and to expedite complete restoration, anticipated the regular work of the legislature by creating congressional districts, in order that Georgia's representatives might be chosen at that election.[4]

One thing now remained to be done before the President would withdraw federal power and leave the state to its own government, viz., ratification of the Thirteenth Amendment. The legislature elected on November 15th assembled on December 4th.[5] The provisional governor, according to the President's directions,[6] laid the Thirteenth Amendment before it.   The Amendment was ratified on December 9th.[7] After this the provisional governor was relieved, the governor elect was inaugurated (December 14th), and the President sent a courteous message of recognition to the latter.[8]

Thus the President, having reconstructed the state government, had restored Georgia to statehood so far as its internal government was concerned.   There remained only the admission of its representatives to Congress to complete the restoration.

[1] J. C., 1865, p. 8.   [2] *Ibid.*, pp. 17, 18.

[3] *Ibid.*, p. 234. The ordinance to this effect was passed only after a hard fight, and after a telegraphic warning from the President that if it failed the state would fail of restoration. See S. D., 39th Congress, 1st session, no. 26, p. 81.

[4] J. C., 1865, pp. 18 and 28.   [5] S. J., 1865–6, p. 3.

[6] S. D., 39th Congress, 1st session, no. 26, p. 95.   [7] S. L., 1865, p. 313.

[8] M. F. U., December 19 and 26, 1865.

CHAPTER II

THE JOHNSON GOVERNMENT

FROM the conduct of the state governments formed in Georgia and the other southern states under the direction of President Johnson, the public opinion of the North drew conclusions regarding three things; the disposition of the people represented by those governments toward the emancipated slaves, their attitude toward the cause for which they had fought, and their feeling toward the power which had subdued them. This chapter treats the Johnson government of Georgia from the same points of view.

Whatever may have been the prevailing disposition of the white people toward the slaves while slavery flourished, shortly before the close of the war that disposition was characterized by benevolence and gratitude. In spite of the opportunities of escape, and of plunder and other violence, offered by the times, the slaves had acted with singular faithfulness and devotion.[1] The gratitude of their masters even went so far as to propose plans for the general education of the negroes.[2]

The close of the war and the advent of emancipation produced a change in the conduct of the negroes, which in time produced a change in the attitude of the white people. The negroes, from the talk which they heard and did not understand, and from their ignorant imaginations, conceived strange ideas of emancipation. They supposed it meant

---

[1] See Jenkins' message to the legislature, M. F. U., December 19, 1865.

[2] K. K. R., vol. 6, p. 320 (testimony of John B. Gordon).

16

governmental bounty, idleness, and wealth.   They abandoned
their work, wandered about the country, collected in towns
—in short, manifested a general restlessness and demoralization. This caused alarm and apprehension among the
white people. There were other causes of friction between
the two races. Many negroes, on discovering that they were
free, assumed what are known as "airs;" and then as now,
among things intolerable to a southern white man a "sassy
nigger" held a curious pre-eminence. The airs of the negro
and the wrath of the white man were both augmented by
officious members of the Freedmen's Bureau. Moreover,
because the negroes had gained by the humiliation of the
South, they received a share of the venom of defeat. Another element of discord was furnished by a particular part
of the white population, the so-called poor whites. These
saw in the new *protégés* of the United States not only a rival
laboring class, but a menace to their social position, and
hence assumed an attitude of jealousy and hatred. Such
were the conditions favorable to social disturbance which
followed emancipation. In the latter part of 1865 they had
already begun to produce their natural result, Violent en-
counters between negroes and white men (in which the
latter were almost always the aggressors) were noticeably
frequent.[1]

To this social demoralization was added economic distress
and perplexity. The devastation of the war had fallen with
especial severity upon Georgia. Worse still, the people
seemed unable to repair the damage or to return to pro-
ductive activity. Planters seemed unable to adapt themselves to the new economic conditions. Slavery, the system
which they understood, was gone; they used the new system with little success, all the less because of the restlessness of the negroes.

[1] Report of Carl Schurz on conditions in the South, made in December, 1865.
S. D., 39th Congress, 2d session, no. 2.

Such were the conditions and dangers with which the Johnson government had to deal as it best could. It was believed by northern statesmen that the situation would be mastered by enfranchising the negroes and investing them with a citizenship exactly equal to that of white persons.[1] The Georgia constitution of 1865 made it clear that the Georgia law-makers were not disciples of that school. That constitution confined the electoral franchise to " free white male citizens." [2] It ordered the legislature at its first session " to provide by law for the government of free persons of color," for " guarding them and the state against any evil that may arise from their sudden emancipation," and " for the regulation of their transactions with citizens ;" also " to create county courts with jurisdiction in criminal cases excepted from the exclusive jurisdiction of the Superior [county] Court, and in civil cases whereto free persons of color may be parties," and to make rules " prescribing in what cases their testimony shall be admitted in the courts." [3]

The legislation enacted in 1866 in the interest of the public peace and order consisted of—

1. An apprentice law. By this it was made the duty of the judges of the county courts to bind out minors whose parents were dead or unable to support them as apprentices until the age of twenty-one. A master receiving an apprentice under this law was to teach him a trade. furnish him food, clothes, and medicine, teach him habits of industry, honesty, and morality, teach him to read the English language, and govern him with humanity. On default of any of these requirements a master was to be fined. The judge having charge of this law might, on application from an apprentice or an apprentice's friend, dissolve the contract

---

[1] Report of Carl Schurz on conditions in the South, made in December, 1865. S. D., 39th Congress, 2d session, no. 2.

[2] Art. v, sect. 1, § 1.   [3] Art. ii, sec. 5, § 5.

on account of cruelty on the part of the master. An apprentice at the end of his term was entitled to an allowance from the master "with which to begin life." The amount was left to the master's generosity, but if he offered less than $100 the apprentice might complain to the court, which should then fix the amount.[1]

2. A vagrancy law. Vagrancy was defined in the usual language of our criminal codes. The penalty was heavier than these usually provide, because the need of suppressing the vice was more urgent than usual. A vagrant might be fined or imprisoned at the discretion of the court, or sentenced to labor on the public works for not more than one year; or he might, at the discretion of the court "be bound out to some person for a time not more than one year, upon such valuable consideration as the court may prescribe."[2]

3. Alterations in the penal laws. These alterations were of two contrasting kinds. The penalty for burglary in the night, arson, horse stealing and rape was changed from long imprisonment[3] to death,[4] which, however, might be in every case commuted to life imprisonment.[5] On the other hand, several hundred crimes, including all the species of larceny except that mentioned above, were reduced from felonies to misdemeanors, and the penalties from imprisonment in the penitentiary to fine, imprisonment in the county jail, or whipping, at the discretion of the court.[6] This mitigation of punishment was made in consideration of the negroes' ignorance of the nature of their offences, due to the fact that these had before been punished by their masters and not by

[1] S. L., 1865–66, p. 6.   [2] S. L., 1865–66, p. 234.

[3] Before, the maximum penalty for rape, arson, and burglary in the night had been imprisonment for 20 years, and for horse stealing imprisonment for 5 years

[4] S. L., 1865–66, p. 232; 1866, p. 151.   [5] Ibid., 1866, p. 150.

[6] Ibid., 1865–66, p. 233.

the law.   Probably the capacity of the penitentiary was also considered.

To facilitate the transition from the old labor system to the new by remedying in some degree the instability of the labor supply, the legislature made it a crime to employ any servant during the term for which he had contracted to work for another, or to induce a servant to quit the service of an employer before the close of the period contracted for.[1]

Regarding the civil rights and relations of the negroes the following legislation was passed:

1. A law in these words:

That persons of color shall have the right to make and enforce contracts; to sue, be sued; to be parties and give evidence; to inherit; to purchase, lease, sell, hold and convey real and personal property; and to have full and equal benefit of all laws and proceedings for the security of person and estate; and shall not be subject to any other or different punishment, pain or penalty for the commission of any act or offence than such as are prescribed for white persons committing like acts or offences.[2]

2. A provision, implied in the law above quoted, that negroes were to be held competent witnesses in all courts in cases, civil or criminal, whereto persons of color should be parties.[3]

3. Certain provisions for establishing among the negroes the regular relations between husband and wife, parent and child, in place of the irregular relations which had prevailed under slavery.[4]

4. The prohibition of marriage between negroes and white persons.[5]

This last provision, and also the exclusion of the testimony of negroes from cases whereto a colored person was not party, are of social rather than legal importance, since their effect was to separate the two races, but not to deprive the negroes of the equal protection and benefit of the law.   They

[1] S. L., 1866, p. 153.   [2] Ibid., 1865–66, p. 239.
[3] Ibid.   [4] Ibid., p. 240.   [5] Ibid., 241.

were like the school law, which provided that only "free white inhabitants of the state" were entitled to instruction in the public schools.[1]

The Johnson government thus assigned to the negroes a position of political incapacity, social inferiority, but equality of civil rights. This plan was very remote from that in favor in the North, but it is not thereby condemned. As to the measures of the Johnson government for remedying industrial distress and guarding against social dangers, we search them in vain for the inhuman harshness to the negroes which they were reputed to embody. This legislation of Georgia was more favorable to the negroes than that of the other Johnson governments. But the North looked at the conquered South as a whole, and if the difference of the laws of Georgia from those of other states was noticed, it was quickly forgotten. To northern public opinion the scheme for the treatment of the negroes embodied in the Georgia laws, even if its mildness had been recognized, would have been a cause of indignation. This was the consummate hour of a humanitarian enthusiasm sprung from forty years of anti-slavery agitation, and now intensified by the passions of the war. In such an hour a plan which frankly denied to the negroes political and social equality was looked upon as an offence against justice and humanity. The Georgia law-makers had sought for a plan to meet immediate necessities, not a plan for the elevation of the black race. To demand that Georgia, stricken and menaced as she was, should pass by the needs of the present and enter upon a vague scheme of philanthropy, was unreasonable. It was just as unreasonable to conclude from the course which Georgia took, that the black race in Georgia would be forever held down, or that positive encouragement would be

[1] S. L., 1866, p. 59.

withheld as time went on.   Nevertheless the public opinion of the North made this demand and drew these conclusions.

Having stated the attitude of the Johnson government to the emancipated slave, we next come to its attitnde toward the fallen Confederacy and toward the federal government. And with reference to this subject the following facts are to be noticed :

1. Almost the first act of the constitutional convention was to vote a memorial to the President in behalf of Jefferson Davis.[1]

2. The convention, instead of declaring that the ordinance of secession was an act of illegality and error, and was null and void, laconically declared it " repealed." [2]

3. The convention anticipated the function of the legislature in order to provide pensions for the wounded Confederate soldiers and for widows of the dead.[3]

Through the legislature Georgia showed herself equally frank in expressing affection and regret for the lost cause, and equally wanting in an attitude of humility to the federal government—or at least to the dominant party in Congress. On the recommendation of the governor she rejected the Fourteenth Amendment by an almost unanimous vote, largely because of the disabilities it imposed on the leaders of the Confederacy.[4]   Instead of remaining a humbly silent spectator of the controversy between the President and Congress, she boldly thanked the President for his " regard for the constitutional rights of states," and for " the determined will that says to a still hostile faction of her recent foes, ' Thus far shalt thou go and no farther.   Peace, be still.' " [5]

[1] J. C., 1865, p. 16.   [2] *Ibid.*, p. 17.   [3] *Ibid.*, 137.

[4] S. L., 1866, p. 216.   For the governor's message and the report of the committee to which the amendment was referred, see A. A. C., 1865, p. 352.   For a further expression of public opinion, see Atlanta *New Era*, October 19, 1866.

[5] S. L., 1865–66, p. 315.

She continued to provide for the unfortunate champions of the Confederacy, characterizing this action as " a holy and patriotic duty." [1]   She extended expressions of " sincerest condolence and warmest sympathy" to the illustrious state prisoner, Jefferson Davis, declaring that her " warmest affections cluster[ed] around the fallen chief of a once dear but now abandoned cause." [2]

These acts and resolutions expressed through the government the spirit which was found among the people by direct observers—a spirit of submission to irresistible force, in some cases sullen, in most cases unrepentant.[3]   At that time the absence of that spirit would have been extraordinary. But the public opinion of the North regarded it not as the aftermath of war, which would soon pass, but as a spirit which, if left undisciplined, would break out in another war.

This belief, and the belief that the negroes were destined by the southern governments to suffer injustice and debasement, and that the ballot was their only salvation, gave rise to two corresponding purposes — to chasten the rebellious spirit of the South, and to invest the negroes with the voting franchise by force.   To destroy the state governments of the South and rebuild them on a basis of negro suffrage would accomplish both these purposes.   This plan was also supported for the sake of a third purpose, viz., to secure for the Republican party the votes of the negroes.   There were thus three classes of men bent on abolishing the Johnson government.   We may call them the Disciplinarians, the Humanitarians, and the Republican Politicians.

[1] S. L., 1865–66, p. 14, and S. L., 1866, p. 143.
[2] S. L., 1866, p. 219.   [3] Report of Carl Schurz above cited.

CHAPTER III

CONGRESSIONAL DELIBERATIONS AND ACTIONS CONCERN-
ING THE JOHNSON GOVERNMENTS, ENDING IN THE
RECONSTRUCTION ACTS OF 1867

WHEN Congress met on December 4, 1865, President
Johnson informed it of the measures he had taken for restoring the southern states and of the conditions he had required as necessary to restoration. He emphasized the
requirement that the Thirteenth Amendment be ratified
(which, as stated in Chapter I, was complied with in Georgia
five days later).

It is not too much to ask [he said], in the name of the whole people, that, on
the one side, the plan of restoration shall proceed in conformity with a willingness
to cast the disorders of the past into oblivion; and that, on the other, the evidence
of sincerity in the future maintenance of the Union shall be put beyond any doubt
by the ratification of the proposed amendment. . . . The amendment to the Constitution being adopted, it would remain for the states . . . to resume their places
in the two branches of the national legislature.[1]

That Congress was not entirely pleased with the President's course; that it did not agree with him considering
the adoption of the Thirteenth Amendment, the most that
could be asked of the southern states, and that it did not
intend to give effect to his last suggestion, soon became
apparent. In the Senate, on the day on which the President's message was read, Sumner offered resolutions to the
effect that before the southern states should be admitted to
representation in Congress they must enfranchise "all citizens," establish systems of education open to negroes equally

[1] C. G., 39th Congress, 1st session. Appendix, p. 1.

24

with white people, and choose loyal persons for state and national offices.[1] The resolutions concluded: "That the states cannot be precipitated back to political power and independence, but they must wait until these conditions are in all respects fulfilled."[2]

The House of Representatives, after organizing, immediately proposed to the Senate a joint committee to "inquire into the condition of the states which formed the so-called Confederate States of America, and report whether they, or any of them, are entitled to be represented in either house of Congress." The Senate accepted the proposal, and on December 13 the committee was formed.[3]

Five months passed before the committee reported. During that interval Congress took no action determining the question at issue. A vast number of bills and resolutions was introduced proposing various modes of treatment for the southern states and various theories regarding their status, which are interesting to the historian, but all of which fell by the way. The Freedmen's Bureau Bill, if it had become law during this period, would have implied that in the opinion of Congress the late Confederate States were simply territory of the United States and not states in the Union.[4] But this bill failed to be repassed over the President's veto.[5] The Civil Rights Bill, which became law on April 9, 1866, made it a crime to discriminate against any person on account of his race or color under the alleged authority of any state law or custom, gave the federal judicial authorities power to arrest and punish any person guilty of this offense,

---

[1] One of the Senators elect from Georgia had been Vice-President of the defunct Confederacy.

[2] C. G., 39th Congress, 1st session, p. 2.

[3] R. C., 39th Congress, 1st session, vol. ii, p. iii.

[4] C. G., 39th Congress, 1st session, appendix, p. 82.

[5] C. G., 39th Congress, 1st session, p. 915.

and also gave the federal courts jurisdiction over any case before a state court in which such discrimination was attempted.[1]   This law created entirely new relations between federal and state authority, but since it was passed as an act to enforce the Thirteenth Amendment,[2] and applied to all states alike, it committed Congress to no declaration regarding the status of the southern states.

The joint committee made its long-expected report on April 30, 1866.[3]   A great number of witnesses had been examined regarding conditions in the South, whose testimony fills a large volume and purports to be the basis of the committee's report.   The committee thought that since the Johnson governments had been set up under the military authority of the President and were merely instruments through which he had exercised that power in governing conquered territory, they were not regular state governments.   This belief was confirmed by the fact that the existing state constitutions had been framed by conventions acting under the constant direction of the President, and also by the fact that they had not been submitted to the people for adoption.   The Johnson governments then were not state governments at all, and so could not send representatives to Congress.

The committee appealed less to this constitutional argument than to arguments of policy.   It was willing to grant the " profitless abstraction " that the southern states still remained states.   The people of those states had waged war on the United States.   Though subdued, they were defiant, disloyal, and abusive.   They showed no disposition to abate their hatred for the Union or their affection for the Confederacy.   To accord to such a people entire independence,

[1] U. S. L., vol. 14, p. 27.

[2] Trumbull's speech, C. G., 39th Congress, 1st session, p. 474.

[3] R. C., 39th Congress, 1st session, vol. ii.

taking no measures for security from future danger; to admit their representatives to Congress; to allow conquered enemies "to participate in making laws for their conquerors;" to turn over to the custody of recent enemies the treasury, the army, the whole administration—this would be madness unexampled.

For these reasons the committee recommended a joint resolution and two bills. The resolution proposed an amendment to the Constitution forbidding any state to abridge the civil rights of citizens of the United States, or to deny to any person the equal protection of the laws, providing that a state which withheld the electoral franchise from negroes should suffer a deduction from its Congressional representation, and providing that until 1870 all adherents to the Confederacy should be excluded from voting for members of Congress and for Presidential electors. The first of the two bills was to enact "that whenever the above recited amendment [should] have become a part of the Constitution of the United States, and any state lately in insurrection [should] have ratified the same, and [should] have modified its constitution and laws in accordance therewith," then its representatives might be admitted to Congress. The second bill was to make ineligible to office under the United States men who had been prominent in the service of the Confederacy.

A minority of the committee took issue with the majority on both its legal and its political views. The states under consideration, said the minority, had never gone out of the Union; therefore, being states of the Union, Congress could not lawfully deprive them of their rights as states. That the Johnson governments were only the machinery of military occupation, set up by the conquering general, was denied.

We know [said the minority report] that [the southern states] have governments completely organized, with legislative, executive, and judicial functions. We know that they are now in successful operation; no one within their limits questions their legality, or is denied their protection. How they were formed, under what auspices they were formed, are inquiries with which Congress has no concern.

A state is under no restriction as to the mode of altering its constitution; if it chooses to receive assistance from the President, or any one else, the validity of the amended constitution is not affected.

To the statement of the majority regarding the disposition of the southern people, the minority opposed the high authority of General Grant. In an official report he had said :

I am satisfied that the mass of thinking men of the South accept the present situation of affairs in good faith. . . . [They] are in earnest in wishing to do what they think is required by the government . . . and if such a course was pointed out they would pursue it in good faith.

The right way in which to deal with the southern people was, then, to conciliate them, as the President had tried to do, not to perpetuate their hostility.

If Congress adopted the program recommended by the majority, said the minority, it would repudiate its own solemn declaration made in 1861,

that this war is not waged upon our part in any spirit of oppression, nor purpose of overthrowing or interfering with the rights or established institutions of those states, but to defend and maintain the supremacy of the Constitution, and to preserve the Union, with all the dignity, equality, and rights of the several states unimpaired.[1]

The proposed provisions regarding ineligibility would dishonor the government by annulling the pardons granted by the President. Further, the program contradicted itself, since it proposed to treat the southern communities as states, in submitting a constitutional amendment to them, while at the same time imposing on them conditions to which a state could not lawfully be subjected.

[1] Senate resolution (by Andrew Johnson), C. G., 37th Congress, 1st session, pp. 243, 265; House resolution (by Crittenden), *ibid.*, pp. 209, 222.

After a debate of which these two opposing reports are a convenient summary, Congress adopted the program of the committee. The joint resolution, changed into a form embodying the present Fourteenth Amendment, was passed on June 13, 1866.[1] The two bills proposed were taken up, but Congress adjourned without bringing them to a final vote, leaving the South to be regulated during the recess by the Civil Rights Act, and by an act, passed over the President's veto on July 16, embodying in a less drastic form the provisions of the Freedmen's Bureau Bill which had failed in February.[2]

When Congress met in December, 1866, the same voluminous mass of reconstruction proposals and declaratory resolutions appeared in both houses as at the last session. But the denunciation of the President and of the Johnson governments was more emphatic in these bills and resolutions, as well as in the debates. Sumner proposed a resolution to this effect:

That all proceedings with a view to reconstruction originating in executive power are in the nature of usurpation; that this usurpation becomes especially offensive when it sets aside the fundamental truths of our institutions; that it is shocking to common sense when it undertakes to derive new governments from the hostile populations which have just been engaged in armed rebellion, and that all governments having such origin are necessarily illegal and void.[3]

Another resolution proposed that the committee of the House on territories be instructed to take steps for organizing the districts known as Virginia, North Carolina, etc., into states. Cullom said in a speech:

During the last session of this Congress we sent to the country a proposed amendment to the Constitution. . . . . The people of the rebel states by their pretended legislatures are treating it with scorn and contempt. . . . . It is time, sir, that the people of the states were informed in language not to be misunder-

---

[1] U. S. L., vol. 14, p. 358.   [2] *Ibid.*, p. 173.

[3] U. S. Senate Journal, 39th Congress, 2d session, p. 21.

stood that the people who saved this country are going to reconstruct it in their own way, the opposition of rebels to the contrary notwithstanding.[1]

Another fact which appeared prominently in the speeches and resolutions of this session was the growing fear, real or assumed, that freedmen and loyal persons in the South were in mortal danger. Bills for their protection were introduced by the dozen.

Shall we shut our eyes [said a speaker] to the abuse and murders of loyal men in the South, and the continued destruction of their property by wicked men, and give them no means of protection?[2]

Stevens exclaimed that the United States would be disgraced unless Congress proceed[ed] at once to do something to protect these people from the barbarians who [were] daily murdering them; who [were] murdering the loyal whites daily, and daily putting into secret graves not only hundreds but thousands of the colored people.[3]

At first the lower house resumed its consideration of the bills recommended at the last session by the joint committee. But early in February, 1867, these were dropped in favor of a new bill. This was the Reconstruction Bill which became law on March 2. It provided that the South should be divided into five districts, each to comprise the territory of one or more of the southern states. The President should assign to each district a military officer not below the rank of brigadier-general, and should detail for his use a sufficient military force. The duties of these officers should be " to protect all persons in their rights of person and property, to suppress insurrection, disorder and violence, and to punish, or cause to be punished, disturbers of the public peace and criminals." To this end they might either allow local courts to exercise their usual jurisdiction or organize special military courts, for the procedure of which a few general regulations were provided in the bill. Until the states should be by law restored to the Union, the governments existing in

[1] C. G., 39th Congress, 2d session, p. 814.   [2] *Ibid.*
[3] C. G., 39th Congress, 2d session, p. 251.

them were declared " provisional only, and in all respects subject to the paramount authority of the United States, at any time to abolish, modify, control or suspend the same."

In section 5 of this bill were stated the conditions upon which the southern states might regain their places in the Union. In each of them a constitutional convention should be elected. For members of this convention all male " citizens " of the voting age should vote, except those excluded from office by the pending Fourteenth Amendment. These were forbidden to sit in the convention or to vote for delegates. The convention thus formed should frame a new constitution, which should give the franchise to all persons qualified to vote for delegates by the present bill. The constitution should be submitted to the people of the state for ratification, and to Congress for approval. When these should have been received, and when the legislature elected under the new constitution should have ratified the Fourteenth Amendment, then Congress should pass an act admitting the reconstructed state to Congressional representation, and the present law should cease to operate in that state.[1]

The principle of this bill was the same as that of the reconstruction measures first undertaken at the suggestion of the joint committee, namely the punishment of an enemy. The debate in the House was opened by a felicitous quotation from Vattel on the public law applicable to the case of a conquered enemy.[2] The punishment here provided was, however, more severe than that first proposed. The former program was designed to offer to the states the alternative of adopting the Fourteenth Amendment or remaining out of the Union and under the Freedman's Bureau—which was, indeed, regarded as a very obnoxious alternative. But the present bill required them not only to ratify the amend-

[1] U. S. L., vol. 14, p. 428.
[2] C. G., 39th Congress, 2d session, p. 1076.

ment, but to adopt new constitutions, elect new governments, enfranchise the negroes, and disfranchise their most prominent and respected citizens; and meanwhile imposed upon them not simply a bureau, to interfere in individual cases, but the virtually absolute rule of a military governor.

This bill was passed over Johnson's veto on March 2, 1867. On March 23 a supplementary act was passed, providing means for executing section 5 of the preceding act. The initiative in calling the constitutional conventions, instead of being left to the states, to be exercised or not, as they chose, was now assigned to the military governor. He, with the assistance of such boards of registry as he might create, was directed to register all persons qualified to vote for delegates. He should then fix the number of delegates and arrange the plan of representation, set the day for election and summon the convention.[1]

A third reconstruction act was passed on July 19, 1867. It is unnecessary to discuss it, since it was only explanatory of the acts of March 2 and 23, and added nothing which needs mention here to their provisions.[2]

Were the Reconstruction Acts constitutional? Since the Supreme Court has failed, either voluntarily or otherwise, to decide every case brought before it depending upon this question,[3] reasoning is not rendered idle by authority. The Supreme Court has indeed expressed a definite opinion on the subject, but has given no decision.

The opinion referred to was expressed in the case of Texas *versus* White.[4] The Court said:

These new relations [namely, those created by the civil war] imposed new duties

---

[1] U. S. L., vol. 15, p. 2.   [2] *Ibid.*, p. 14.

[3] Mississippi *versus* Johnson, 4 Wallace, 475; Georgia *versus* Stanton, 6 Wallace, 51; *Ex parte* McCardle, 6 Wallace, 324, and 7 Wallace, 512.

[4] 7 Wallace, 700.

upon the United States. The first was that of suppressing the rebellion. The next was that of re-establishing the broken relations of the states with the Union. The authority for the performance of the first had been found in the power to suppress insurrection and to carry on war; for the performance of the second, authority was derived from the obligation of the United States to guarantee to every state a republican form of government.

This the Court considered good authority for the passage of the Reconstruction Acts. Most of the advocates of the acts based them upon this theory.

Now, upon that clause of Article IV., Section 4, of the Constitution which says: "The United States shall guarantee to every state in this Union a republican form of government," the *Federalist* remarks:

It may possibly be asked whether [this clause] may not become a pretext for alterations in the state governments without the concurrence of the states themselves. . . . But the authority extends no further than to a *guarantee* [the *Federalist's* italics] of a republican form of government, which supposes a pre-existing government of the form which is to be guaranteed.[1]

The intention of the clause, says the *Federalist* in the same paper, is simply to guard " against aristocratic or monarchic innovations." To one not interested in establishing the constitutionality of the Reconstruction Acts, it seems indisputable that the clause is rightly interpreted by the *Federalist*. Story accepts this interpretation as a matter of course.[2] Cooley groups the clause with that which forbids the states to grant titles of nobility.[3] If this interpretation is correct, then the guarantee clause gives no authority for destroying a state government of a republican form and substituting another.

There is, however, a constitutional basis for the Reconstruction Acts. It is the war power of Congress.

If a section of the people of a state rebels against the gov-

[1] The *Federalist*, no. 43.

[2] Story on the Constitution, chap. 41 (4th edition).

[3] Cooley on the Constitution, p. 23 (4th edition).

ernment, the resulting contest is not a war, in the sense of international law. But as it may assume the physical character of a war, so it may call into existence the rights and customs incident to war. Upon this principle the federal government acquired the rights of war in the contest of 1861-1865.[1] Now the rights of war do not end with military operations; one of these rights is the right of the victorious party, after an unconditional surrender, to occupy the territory of the defeated party, to govern or punish the people as it sees fit. If the United States government acquired the rights of war, this right was included. The close of a war is not simultaneous with the cessation of fighting. The surrender of the southern armies was an important incident in the civil war; it was not the end. If the federal government had the rights of war before this incident, it had them after.

The United States government might therefore say to the persons composing the military power which it had subdued: As the terms of war, you are to be governed by military government. If the persons against whom this sentence is assumed to have been pronounced formed the majority of the population of a state, one result of the sentence would be to suspend independent state government. The United States government might choose another punishment. It might say to the lately hostile persons: We forbid you to participate in the federal government. If the persons so sentenced form the majority of the population of a state, that state can send no representatives to Congress while the sentence remains. These sentences might be imposed permanently or only until such time as the people sentenced should fulfil certain demands—hold certain conventions, pass certain laws, adopt certain resolutions in certain ways. The federal government can thus effect through

---

[1] Prize Cases, 2 Black, 687.

its war powers what it cannot effect through any power to interfere directly with a state government. It had no right to reconstruct the government of Maine in 1865, because Maine had no body of people over whom the federal government could exercise war powers. It had the right to reconstruct the government of Georgia, because nine-tenths of the people of Georgia were lawfully at its mercy as a conqueror.

Even if it be admitted, however, that the federal government had the power described, it may still be argued that the Reconstruction Acts are not legally justified. A conqueror has a right to govern a conquered people as he pleases and as long as he pleases; he also has a right to alter his mode of treatment and substitute another mode. But after he has imposed certain terms as final, after the requirements of these terms have been complied with, after he has restored the conquered people to their normal position and rights and has unmistakably terminated the relation of conqueror to conquered—then his rights of war are at an end. It may be argued that this was the case when the Reconstruction Acts were passed. It may be argued that in December, 1865, the federal government had, through the President, terminated its capacity as a conqueror, and could regain that capacity only by another war; that after that termination it had no more power to reconstruct Georgia than to reconstruct Maine.

This argument is irrefutable if we assume that the President had full power to act for the federal government in the disposition of the defeated Secessionists, and that therefore his acts of 1865 were the acts of the federal government. In case of an international war, which is closed by a treaty, the President may if supported by the Senate) act finally for the federal government, and estop that government (so far as international law is concerned) from further action. But at the close of a civil war he cannot exercise his diplomatic power.   The disposition of the defeated people in this case falls to the legislative branch of the government.

If the President had pardoned a great majority of the Secessionists, that fact perhaps might have legally estopped Congress from passing the Reconstruction Acts. These acts were a war punishment, and a pardon cuts off further punishment.[1]   But the total number of persons who received amnesty under the proclamation of May 29, 1865, was 13,596,[2] which was of course only a small fraction of the Secessionist population.

The passage of the Reconstruction Acts may thus be regarded, from a legal point of view, as simply the substitution of one method of treating the defeated enemy for another. The change was from mildness to harshness.   It was doubly bitter to the defeated enemy, after he had been led to believe that his punishment was over, to be subjected to a worse one.   But these are not legal considerations.

That the Reconstruction Acts required communities not states to ratify a constitutional amendment did not affect their legality.   That an amendment depended for its validity on such ratification might make the amendment void (though even from this result there is a means of escape in the theory of relation, to be mentioned later), but that would not affect the act requiring the ratification.   That this requirement was not made with the exclusive purpose of obtaining votes for the passage of the amendment is shown by a resolution introduced into the House of Representatives on July 21, 1867, which reads:

Resolved, That in ratifying amendments to the Constitution of the United States . . . the said several states . . . are wholly incapable either of accepting or rejecting any such amendment so as to bind the loyal states of the Union, . . . and that when any amendment . . . shall be adopted by three-fourths of the states

[1] *Ex parte* Garland, 4 Wallace, 333.

[2] Archives of the Department of State, Washington.

recognized by the Congress as lawfully entitled to do so, . . . the same shall become thereby a part of the Constitution.[1]

What virtues the Reconstruction Acts had besides legal regularity will be discussed later.

[1] C. G., 39th Congress, 2d session, p. 615. For other expressions of the same doctrine, see Cullom's speech, *ibid.*, p. 814; Sumner's resolutions, C. G., 39th Congress, 1st session, p. 2; Sumner's resolutions, C. G., 40th Congress, 2d session, p. 453.

CHAPTER IV

THE ADMINISTRATIONS OF POPE AND MEADE

In the Third Military District, of which Georgia was a part, the Reconstruction Acts were administered from April 1, 1867, to January 6, 1868, by General Pope, and from January 6 to July 30, 1868, by General Meade.[1] The present chapter will describe, first, the manner in which these men conducted the political rebuilding of Georgia, and second, the manner in which they governed during this process.

On April 8 Pope issued his first orders regarding the registration of voters. The three officers commanding respectively in the sub-districts of Georgia, Florida and Alabama were directed to divide the territory under them into registration districts, and for each of these to appoint a board of registry consisting as far as possible of civilians.[2] On May 2 the scheme of districts for Georgia was published. The state was divided into forty-four districts of three counties each, and three districts of a city each. For each district the names of two white registrars were announced, and each of these pairs was ordered to complete the board by selecting a negro colleague. The compensation of registrars was to be from fifteen cents to forty cents for every name registered, varying according to the density or sparseness of the population. It was made the duty of registrars to explain to those unused to the enjoyment of suffrage the nature of this function. After the lists were complete they were to be published for ten days.[3]

[1] G. O. H., 1867, no. 18 and 104; 1868, no. 55; G. O. T. M. D., 1867, no. 1; 1868, no. 3 and 108.

[2] G. O. T. M. D., 1867, no. 5.

[3] *Ibid.*, 1867, no. 20.

The unsettled condition of the negro population suggested to Pope the possibility that many negroes would lose their right to vote by change of residence. He therefore ordered on August 15 that persons removing from the district where they were registered should be furnished by the board of registry with a certificate of registration, which should entitle them to vote anywhere in the state.[1]

The election for deciding whether a constitutional convention should be held, and for choosing delegates in case the affirmative vote prevailed, was ordered to begin on October 29 and to continue three days. Registrars were ordered to revise their lists during the fortnight preceding the election, to erase names wrongly registered, and to add the names of persons entitled to be registered. The boards of registry were to act as judges of election, but registrars who were candidates for election were forbidden to serve in the districts where they sought election.[2]

The election was to occupy the last three days of October. On October 30 Pope extended the time to the night of November 2, in order to give the negroes ample opportunity to vote, which in their inexperience they might otherwise fail to do.[3]

After the election the following figures were announced:[4]

Number of registered voters in Georgia 188,647
Of these the negroes numbered....................... 93,457
    "   the white men[5]........................... 95,214
Number of votes polled............................. 106,410
    "   "   for a convention 102,283
    "   "   against a convention 4,127

The delegates elected were ordered to meet in conven-

[1] G. O. T. M. D., 1867, no. 50.   [2] *Ibid*, 1867, no. 69.   [3] *Ibid.*, 1867, no. 83.

[4] *Ibid.*, 1867, no. 89. Also see Pope's Report, in R. S. W., 40th Congress, 2d session, vol. i, p. 320.

[5] There is a slight inaccuracy in the official figures.

tion on December 9th.[1]   On that day the convention met in
Atlanta.   Its business was not completed until the middle of
March in the following year.   The constitution which it
framed more than met the demands of the Reconstruction
Acts.   A single citizenship was established for all residents
of the state, in language borrowed from the Fourteenth
Amendment to the federal Constitution.[2]   Legislation on
the subject of social status of citizens was forever prohibited.[3]
The electoral right was given to all male persons born or
naturalized in the United States who should have resided
six months in Georgia.[4]   Electors were privileged from
arrest (except for treason, felony or breach of the peace) for
five days before, during, and for two days after, elections, and
the legislature was ordered to provide such other means for
the protection of electors as might be necessary.[5]   Other
provisions presumably acceptable to northern sentiment were
the prohibition of whipping as a penalty for crime,[6] and the
command that the legislature should create a system of public schools free to all children of the state.[7]

By an ordinance of the convention, made valid by being
embodied in military orders, April 20, 1868, was appointed
for the submission of the new constitution to popular vote,
and also for the election of members of Congress and officers
of the new state government.[8]   This election resulted in the
adoption of the constitution by a majority of 17,699 votes,
and in the election of a governor (Rufus B. Bullock by name),
a legislature, and a full delegation to the lower house of Congress.[9]   The remaining requirement of the Reconstruction

[1] G. O. T. M. D., 1867, no. 89.

[2] Georgia Constitution of 1868, art. i, sec. i.   [3] Ibid., art. i, sect. xi.

[4] Ibid., art. ii, sect. ii.   [5] Ibid., art. ii, sect. vii, § 10.

[6] Ibid., art. i, sect. xxii.   [7] Ibid., art. vi, sect. i.

[8] G. O. T. M. D., 1868, no. 39 and 40.

[9] Ibid., no. 76, 90 and 93.   Also, E. D., 40th Congress 2d session, no. 300.

Acts was that the new legislature convene and ratify the
Fourteenth Amendment. This transaction will be reserved
for the next chapter.

General Pope was inspired by the ideas and emotions from
which reconstruction had sprung. He was an ardent friend
of the reconstruction measures. He was convinced of the
importance of suppressing the old political leaders in his
district. He held with enthusiasm the optimistic views prev-
alent in the North regarding the negroes. Their recent progress in "education and knowledge," he said, was "marvel-
lous," and if continued, in five years the intelligence of the
community would shift to the colored portion.[1] The pur-
port of his orders, the didactic style in which they are
couched, the declarations of his principles which frequently
accompany these orders, indicate the spirit in which he
administered the office of military governor.

Most of the official acts of Pope concerned either the
enforcement of obedience and the suppression of disobedi-
ence to the letter and spirit of the Reconstruction Acts, or
the protection and promotion of the present interests of the
freedmen.

In assuming command he announced that in the absence
of special orders all persons holding office under the state
government would be permitted to retain their positions
until the expiration of their terms. Their successors, however, were to be appointed by Pope alone; no elections
should be held in the state except those required by Congress. The general expressed the hope that no necessity for
interference in the regular operation of the state government
would arise. It could arise, he said, only from the failure
of state tribunals to do equal justice to all persons.[2] A few

[1] Pope's Report in R. S. W., 40th Congress, 2d session, vol. i, p. 320.
[2] G. O. T. M. D., 1867, no. 1.

weeks later he announced that this necessity would also arise if any state officer interfered with or opposed the reconstruction measures ; such an officer, it was " distinctly announced," would be deposed.[1] Governor Jenkins, on April 10, had issued a letter to the public, advising them to abstain from registering and voting under the Reconstruction Acts. Pope had excused him with a lecture, and then issued the order referred to, to make clear that no more advice of that sort from state officers would be permitted.[2] Opposition to reconstruction by state officers was declared to include also the awarding of state printing to newspapers which opposed reconstruction, and it was ordered that thereafter the state's patronage should be given only to loyal papers.[3] Another measure to the same end was the order that no state court should entertain any action against any person for any acts done under the military authority.[4] But while opposition by state officers was thus dealt with, freedom of public opinion was emphatically declared. The declaration accompanied a public reprimand administered to the post commander at Mobile for interference with a newspaper.[5]

The careful consideration for the needs of the freedmen shown in the general's method of forming the boards of registry, in his instructions to the registrars, in his provision of certificates of registration to migrating citizens, and in his extension of the time of election, has been pointed out. Of a similar character was the warning to employers that any attempt to prevent laborers from voting, or to influence their votes by docking wages, threats, or any other means, would be severely dealt with.[6]

In his first general orders, as we have said, Pope warned

[1] G. O. T. M. D., 1867, no. 10.

[2] For the correspondence between Jenklns and Pope see A. A. C., 1367, p. 363.

[3] G. O. T. M. D., 1867, no. 49.   [4] *Ibid.*, 1867, no. 45.

[5] *Ibid.*, 1867, no. 28.   [6] *Ibid.*, 1867, no. 69.

the judiciary against racial prejudice. It was probably disregard of this warning which caused the removal of about a dozen judges, justices of the peace, and sheriffs.[1] In the interest of equal justice, Pope also ordered that grand and petit jurors should be selected impartially from the lists of voters registered under the Reconstruction Acts.[2] Besides this general protection, individual relief was given by release from arrest, mitigation of the conditions of confinement, reduction of fines, and other special dispensations.[3] The method of securing justice mentioned in the Act of March 2, 1867, namely by ordering the trial of cases by military commissions, was employed by Pope only once.[4]

Such was the administration of Pope. Its influence on the *personnel* of the state government was large, but was exercised only slightly through removal, chiefly through appointment to fill vacancies. Pope removed about fifteen state officers (almost all of whom were the judicial officers mentioned in the preceding paragraph). He filled about two hundred vacancies.[5] It is significant that a great number of these were caused by resignation. His acts of interference with the action of state officers were few, and with all his zeal for the success of reconstruction, he favored freedom of speech. Nevertheless, his opinions and his personal character, combined with such interference as he did practice, served to gain for him the dislike of the people and the rather unjust reputation of a petty tyrant.

Though Meade lacked Pope's zealous enthusiasm for reconstruction, yet he held much the same opinion as his predecessor regarding the duties with which he was charged. Like Pope, he forbade the bestowal of public patronage on

---

[1] S. O. T. M. D., 1867, *passim.*   [2] G. O. T. M. D., 1867, no. 53.

[3] S. O. T. M. D., 1867, no. 92, 100, 104.   [4] *Ibid.*, 1867, no. 263.

[5] These figures are compiled from the special orders of the Third Military District.

anti-reconstruction newspapers.[1] Like Pope, he thought it his duty to depose state officers who opposed the execution of the Reconstruction Acts. When he assumed command he found the convention at loggerheads with the governor and the state treasurer. The convention had levied a tax to pay its expenses, and pending the collection of it had directed the treasurer to advance forty thousand dollars.[2] The treasurer (Jones by name) declined to do this except on a warrant from the governor, according to the regular practice. Meade requested Jenkins to issue the warrant. Jenkins refused, on the ground that the act would violate the state constitution under which he held office, and that even if it were authorized by the Reconstruction Acts (which he denied), that was an authorization contrary to the Constitution of the United States, upon which he would not act.[3] Thereupon, on January 13, 1868, Meade issued an order by which the governor (designated as the "provisional governor") and the treasurer (also designated as "provisional") were removed and Brigadier-General Ruger and Captain Rockwell "detailed" to act as governor and treasurer respectively.[4] For this act the convention rewarded Meade with a resolution of gratitude.[5] Before the end of the same month the state comptroller and the secretary of state were also removed for ob-

---

[1] G. O. T. M. D., 1868, no. 22.

[2] Ordinance of Dec. 20, 1867, J. C., 1867–8, p. 564.

[3] Avery, *History of Georgia*, p. 378.

[4] G. O. T. M. D., 1868, no. 8. Meade acted with the greatest courtesy, and the relations between him and the officers remained friendly. See Meade's letter to Jenkins, A. A. C., 1867. p. 367. The removal of the treasurer was a formality to preserve the appearance of due discipline; Jones was allowed to retain the money then in the treasury, and to use it in paying the state debt and other expenses of the state government. See his report to the legislature, Sept. 18, 1868; H. J., 1868, p. 359.

[5] J. C., 1867–8, p. 581.

structing reconstruction,[1] and later the mayor and the entire board of aldermen of Columbus shared the same fate.[2]

Toward the freedmen General Meade assumed the attitude of his predecessor. He made similar rules to protect them, in voting, from coercion by employers.[3] On the other hand, observing that too frequent enticement of negroes to political meetings was disturbing industry, he announced that interference of this sort with the rights of employers by political agitators would meet with the same punishment as interference with the rights of freedmen.[4]

Besides following the two policies of suppressing resistance and protecting freedmen, Meade used his power to a great extent simply in the interest of the general welfare. Public peace and order seemed threatened on the eve of the April election. Orders issued on April 4 expressed the belief that there existed a concerted plan, extending widely through the Third District and apparently emanating from a secret organization, to overawe the population and affect elections. Both military and civil officers were ordered to arrest publishers of incendiary articles and to organize special patrols.[5] Troops were distributed so as to command the parts chiefly in danger,[6] and the frequent resignation of office by sheriffs occasioned the order that no more resignations would be permitted, but that the sheriffs must retain their offices and execute the law.[7] By way of benevolent despotism, Meade, at the request of the convention, suspended the operation of the bail process and of the writ of *capias satisfaciendum*, and promulgated the provisions of the new constitution for the relief of debtors until the constitution should become law.[8] Likewise he gave special orders in eight or ten cases sus-

---

[1] G. O. T. M. D., 1868, no. 12 and 17.
[2] S. O. T. M. D., 1868, no. 112.
[3] G. O. T. M. D., 1868, no. 39 and 57.
[4] *Ibid.*, 1868, no. 58.
[5] *Ibid.*, 1868, no. 51.
[6] *Ibid.*, 1868, no. 54.
[7] *Ibid.*, 1868, no. 57.
[8] *Ibid.*, 1868, no. 27 and 37.

pending trials, releasing prisoners, and otherwise preventing hardship or failure of justice. Whereas Pope had convened one military court, Meade convened six,[1] and before these thirty two cases were tried. Meade appointed about seventy state officers and removed about twenty.

These facts show that the two administrations we are considering were alike in policy, and that in action Meade's was the more vigorous. Nevertheless, while Pope was disliked, Meade, thanks to a more attractive character, enjoyed a certain popularity.

Such was the process by which the Disciplinarians, the Humanitarians, and the Republican Politicians hoped to gain their respective purposes. What were the results of the process by the end of the administration of Meade?

For the Disciplinarians they were not encouraging. Military government was received not as discipline but as bullying. The spirit which reconstruction was designed to quell was only embittered; for to those who entertained it reconstruction was not the chastening of the nation, but the domineering of a political party, which it was hoped and believed would soon lose its ascendency.[2]

For the Humanitarians reconstruction had produced written laws regarding equality of civil and political rights, which were deemed a subject of congratulation. Outside the laws they would have found less encouragement. The kindness of the white people toward the negroes had been changed to apprehension by the events of 1865. When the advent of negro suffrage brought the carpet baggers to the South to marshal the negro voters for their own benefit, and when these men began to disturb the negroes by organizing them into mysterious Union Leagues and giving them

[1] G. O. T. M. D., 1868, no. 27, 55, 99, 123, 136, and 148.
[2] M. F. U., Oct. 29, 1867.

indigestible ideas of their rights, apprehension became
alarm. Negroes seized property of all kinds—including
even plantations — by violence, supposing this to be one of
their new rights. Already they had raised a new terror by
crimes against white women, hitherto unknown. Some
thoughtful men believed that the best defence against the
dangers apprehended from the disturbed black population
was kindness and friendly influence.[1] This opinion was not
heard after the arrival of the carpet-baggers; its methods
were then seen to be inadequate. Secret organizations were
formed by white men for protection against the negroes.
These organizations, which sowed the seed of a subsequent
harvest of crime, at first included men of the best character
and of the highest standing.[2] Thus reconstruction, together
with its written laws, had produced conditions which made
the net Humanitarian results doubtful, at least for the
moment.

For the Republican Politicians reconstruction did not produce in Georgia all that was to be desired. When the enter-
prise was first launched some of the white men, though offended, favored accepting the inevitable and endeavoring to
elect good men to the constitutional convention and to the
new state government.[3] Others, carried further by their
anger, determined to take no part in elevating the negroes
and debasing their heroes. Prominent among these, as we
have said, was Governor Jenkins. These men stayed at
home on October 29, 1867, contemptuously ignoring the
"bogus concern called an election," which occurred on that
day.[4] Many of these latter, by the time the "motley crew
assembled at Atlanta" had finished its labors, decided to

[1] Atlanta *New Era*, Nov. 16, 1866; March 13, 1867; March 19, 1867.

[2] Testimony of John B. Gordon, K. K. R., vol. 6, p. 308.

[3] Atlanta *New Era*, March 13, 16 and 30, 1867.

[4] M. F. U., Oct. 29 and Nov. 5, 1867.

follow the example of the former. A convention met at
Macon on December 5, 1867, formed a party, the Georgia
Conservatives, named a ticket, with John B. Gordon at the
head, and began a powerful campaign for the defeat of
negroes and adventurers at the April election.[1] To make an
active fight was recognized as a better course than to stand
in ineffectual scorn.[2] As a result the sweeping victory ex-
pected by the Republican Politicians did not occur in Georgia. A Republican governor was elected; but in the state
senate the seats were equally divided between the Republicans and the Conservatives, in the state house of representatives the Conservatives obtained a large majority, and of
the seven Congressmen elected three were Conservatives.[3]

[1] A. A. C., 1868, p. 309.

[2] Testimony before the reconstruction committee, H. M. D., 40th Congress,
2d session, no. 52, p. 26. See also M. F. U., March 10 and 17, 1867.

[3] Tribune Almanac for 1869, p. 78.

CHAPTER V

THE SUPPOSED RESTORATION OF 1868

THE passage of the Reconstruction Acts of 1867 determined the course of reconstruction, but did not stop discussion. When Congress met in December, 1867, the acts passed continued to be attacked and defended and new bills to be introduced and dropped. But the plan as adopted remained untouched, with one exception.

One of the reasons given by the joint committee on reconstruction for abolishing the Johnson governments was that the Johnson constitutions had not been ratified by popular vote, and therefore did not rest upon the consent of a majority of the people. To avoid a like defect in the new governments the act of March 23 had provided that the new constitutions should be regarded as adopted only if a majority of the registered voters took part in the vote on the question of adoption. At its next session Congress repented of this provision; it was now seen to involve the risk that the opponents of reconstruction in the southern states would defeat the new constitutions by the plan of inaction. This risk should be avoided, since the adoption of a state constitution probably meant the election of a Republican state government, and hence of Republican Senators, as well as Republican Congressional Representatives and Republican Presidential Electors in November, 1868. These advantages would be lost if the new constitutions were defeated. Therefore, by an act which became law on March 11, 1868, the reconstruction legislation was amended so as to provide that elections held under that legislation should be decided by a majority of the votes cast. This act also adopted as part of the general scheme two expedients already employed by Pope in the Third District. That is to say, it provided that any registered voter might vote in any election district in his state, provided he had lived there ten days, and that the elections should be "continued from day to day."[1]

Aside from these alterations, Congress allowed reconstruction to complete its course according to the first plan. Within the first six months of 1868 North Carolina, South Carolina, Louisiana and Florida, besides Georgia, had adopted new constitutions. According to the Act of March 2, 1867, two more steps would complete the process for these states; namely, the ratification by their legislatures of the Fourteenth Amendment, and the declaration "by law" (provided Congress approved the constitutions) that they were entitled to representation in Congress.[2] Congress now decided, instead of waiting for the ratification of the amendment, to pass the declaratory law at once, which should operate as soon as the ratification should have occurred. By this method one act would suffice for all the states which had adopted constitutions.

The bill for this purpose was called the Omnibus Bill. It provided that North Carolina, South Carolina, Georgia, Florida, Louisiana, and also Alabama,[3] should be admitted to representation in Congress as soon as their legislatures elected under the new constitution should have ratified the Fourteenth Amendment, on condition that the provisions of that amendment regarding eligibility to office should at once

[1] U. S. L., vol. 15, Public Laws, p. 41.   [2] See sects. 5 and 6.

[3] The vote in Alabama on the adoption of the constitution resulted in favor of adoption; but less than half of the registered voters voted, and the vote was taken before the passage of the act of March 11, 1868, above mentioned. Excuse was found by the Republican leaders for waiving this irregularity. C. G., 40th Congress, 2d session, p. 2463.

go into operation in those states, and on condition that the constitution of none of them should ever be amended so as to deprive of the right to vote any citizens entitled to that right as the constitutions then stood. A special condition was imposed on Georgia; namely, that Article V., section 17, §§ 1 and 3 of her constitution be declared void by the legislature. A precedent for such a requirement was found in the act of 1821, admitting Missouri to statehood.[1] The bill gave the governors-elect in the states concerned authority to call the legislatures immediately to fulfill the required conditions.[2]

The Omnibus Bill became law on June 25, 1868. On the same day Rufus B. Bullock, the governor-elect of Georgia, issued a proclamation in accordance with the act, summoning the legislature to meet on July 4th.[3]

Now, the Reconstruction Act of July 10th, 1867, had provided as follows:

All persons hereafter elected or appointed to office in said military districts, under any so-called state or municipal authority, or by detail or appointment of the district commanders, shall be required to take......the oath of office prescribed by law for officers of the United States.[4]

On April 15th Meade had announced that in accordance with this provision the members of the legislature to be elected on April 20th would be required to subscribe to the Test Oath. But he was later advised from headquarters, and by certain prominent members of Congress, that the persons contemplated by the act of July 19, 1867, were those elected under the Johnson government, not under the new government; and that therefore the men elected on April

---

[1] C. G., 40th Congress, 2d session, p. 2859 (Trumbull's speech).

[2] U. S. L., vol. 15, Public Acts, p. 73.   [3] S. J., 1868. p. 3.

[4] The Iron Clad or Test Oath, to the effect that the person swearing had never borne arms against the United States, or in any way served the Confederacy. U. S. L., vol. 12, p. 502.

[5] G. O. T. M. D., 1868, no. 61.

20th were not "officers elected under any so-called state authority" in the sense of the act of July 19th. The eligibility of these men, he was told, was to be determined by the provisions of the new constitution and by the Fourteenth Amendment, and they were not required to take the Test Oath.[1] Meade therefore did not enforce his order. But though the new government was exempt from this one requirement of the Reconstruction Acts, it was subject to the provision which said:

......until the people of said rebel states shall be by law admitted to representation in the Congress of the United States, any civil government which may exist therein shall be deemed provisional only, and in all respects subject to the paramount authority of the United States.

Over the new state government, as over the old, Meade would exercise the powers of a district commander until the legislature by complying with the requirements of the Omnibus Act, should have made that act operative.

On June 28 Meade relieved General Ruger of the office of governor and appointed in his place the governor-elect, Bullock, whom he directed to organize the legislature on July 4.[2] When the legislature met on that day, therefore, Bullock called each house to order in turn, and under his direction as chairman the members were sworn in (by the official oath prescribed in the state constitution), and the presiding officers elected.

On July 7 the legislature informed the governor that it was organized and ready to proceed to business. Bullock, instead of replying, wrote to Meade, stating that it was alleged that a number of men seated in the legislature were ineligible to office according to the proposed Fourteenth Amendment, and hence were disqualified from holding their

[1] S. R., 40th Congress, 3d session, no. 192, p. 38. See also C. G., 41st Congress, 1st session, p. 594.

[2] G. O. T. M. D., 1868, no. 98.

seats by the Omnibus Act.[1]   Meade replied on July 8 that
the allegation was serious, and that he would not recognize
as valid any act of the legislature until satisfactory evidence
should be presented that the legislature contained no member who would be disqualified from office by the Fourteenth
Amendment.[2] Bullock sent Meade's letter to the legislature,
and both houses appointed committees to investigate the
eligibility of every member.   These committees reported on
July 17.   The senate committee reported that no senators
were ineligible.   A minority of the committee found, on evidence detailed in its report, that four were ineligible.   After
much debate the majority report was adopted.[3]   The house
committee reported that two representatives were ineligible.
A minority report found three ineligible.   A second minority report found that none were ineligible.   The last was
adopted.[4]

The conclusions of the two houses may be regarded, in
view of these proceedings, with some just suspicion.   Bullock
in informing Meade of them expressed the opinion that the
legislature had failed to furnish the " satisfactory evidence "
upon which Meade had conditioned his recognition.[5]   If
Meade had desired to know the exact truth, he might well
have accepted Bullock's advice and ignored the reports, in-
vestigated the records of the legislators himself, and excluded those whom he found ineligible.   But Meade desired
only to see that the acts of Congress were complied with.
" Satisfactory evidence" was evidence not logically, but
formally satisfactory.   Meade followed the established principle that legislative bodies are the final judges of the eligibility of their members.   He considered the statement of

[1] S. R., 40th Congress, 3d session, no. 192, p. 7.

[2] *Ibid.*   See also H. J., 1868, p. 25.

[3] S. J., 1868, p. 34.   [4] H. J., 1868, pp. 36, 44.

[5] S. R., 40th Congress, 3d session, no. 192, p. 8.

the legislature that its members were all eligible formally satisfactory evidence that the acts of Congress were obeyed. Having this evidence, he refused to interfere further. His decision was influenced partly by reluctance to interfere more than was necessary, and partly by aversion to aiding Bullock to gain a party advantage, which he alleged to be the governor's chief motive in urging the rejection of the reports.[1] He acted with the approval of the general of the army.[2]

He notified the governor that the legislature was legally organized from the date of the adoption of the reports (July 17).[3] Bullock transmitted this message to the legislature on July 21. On that day both houses ratified the Fourteenth Amendment and declared void the sections of the constitution required to be so declared by the Omnibus Act.[4]

As soon as the legislature had performed these acts Georgia was, presumably, according to the acts of Congress, a state of the Union. On July 22 Meade directed all state officers holding by military appointment to turn over their offices to those elected or appointed under the new government.[5] On July 28 orders issued from the headquarters of the army stating that the general commanding in the Third Military District had ceased to exercise authority under the Reconstruction Acts, and that Georgia, Florida and Alabama no longer constituted a military district, but should henceforth constitute an ordinary military circumscription—the Department of the South.[6] On July 22 Bullock, who had up to that time been governor by military appointment, was inaugurated in the regular manner and became governor under the state constitution.[7] On July 25, the seven

---

[1] S. R., 40th Congress, 3d session, no. 192, p. 38.

[2] Ibid.   [3] Ibid., p. 13.   [4] H. J., 1868, p. 52.

[5] G. O. T. M. D., 1868, no. 103.

[6] G. O. H., 1868, no. 55.   [7] H. J., 1868, p. 57.

congressmen-elect from Georgia were seated in the House of Representatives.[1]   The Georgia Senators would doubtless have been seated at this time if they had arrived before the close of the session; but they were elected by the legislature on July 29,[2] two days after Congress adjourned.[3] In view of Georgia's compliance with the Reconstruction Acts and the Omnibus Act, and in view of the various official recognitions that that compliance was complete, there could now be no doubt that her reconstruction was accomplished and her statehood regained.

[1] C. G., 40th Congress, 2d session, pp. 4472, 4499, 4500.

[2] H, J., 1868, p. 104.   [3] C. G., 40th Congress, 2d session, p. 4518.

CHAPTER VI

THE EXPULSION OF THE NEGROES FROM THE LEGISLA-
TURE AND THE USES TO WHICH THIS EVENT
WAS APPLIED

WHEN the Georgia Republicans, or Radicals, as they were
locally called, found that instead of a sweeping victory they
had won only a governorship hemmed in by a hostile legislature, an effort was made, as we have said, to improve their
position through the interference of Meade. Meade refused
to aid them. When, a short time afterwards, federal power,
on which they had hitherto relied, was completely withdrawn,
they seemed left to make the best of an uncomfortable position without any assistance. At this point a god appeared
from the machine.

In the state senate there were three negroes, in the lower
house twenty-five.[1] Their presence was an offense. It was an
offense not merely to the Conservative members. Some of
the Republicans entertained Conservative sentiments and
principles, but supported reconstruction simply in order to
hasten the liberation of the state from Congressional interference.[2] To them as well as to the Conservatives "negro rule"
was obnoxious. Negro rule, so far as it consisted in negro
suffrage, was established by the constitution. But negro
office-holding was not so established expressly. As early as

[1] A. A. C., 1868, p. 312.

[2] The most prominent of these was Ex-Governor Brown. He went as a dele-
gate to the Republican National Convention in 1868, but in a speech there declared his opposition to the granting of political power to the negro. Avery, *History of Georgia*, p. 385.

July 25, 1868, the question, whether negroes were eligible to the legislature, was raised in the state senate.[1]

Legally considered, the question had two sides, each supported by eminent lawyers. For the negroes it was argued that Irwin's Code, which was made part of the law of the state by the constitution,[2] enumerated among the rights of citizens the right to hold office.[3] Negroes were made citizens of equal rights with all other citizens by the new constitution.[4] Therefore they had the right to hold office. It was true that the constitution did not grant the right to hold office to the negroes expressly, as it granted the right to vote; but in view of the fact that the convention which made the constitution was elected by 25,000 white and 85,000 colored men, and that that constitution was adopted by 35,000 white and 70,000 colored men, it would be absurd to suppose that the intent of that instrument was to withhold office from the negroes.[5] On the other side, it was argued that the right to hold office did not belong to every citizen, but only to such citizens as the law specially designated, or to such as possessed it by common law or custom. Irwin's Code could not be cited to prove that negroes had the right, because that law had been enacted before the negroes had been made citizens, and the word *citizens* in it referred to those who were citizens at that time. As the negro had no right to hold office because he was a citizen, and as he could not claim the right from common law or custom, he could obtain it only by specific grant of law. There was no such grant. The argument for the negro was made by the Supreme Court of the state in 1869, the opposing argument by one of the justices of that court in a dissenting opinion.[6]

[1] S. J., 1868, p. 84.   [2] Constitution of 1868, Art. xi, § 3.
[3] Irwin's Code, 1868, § 1648.   [4] Art. i, sec. 2.
[5] This ingenious argument of intent was made by Bullock.   H. J., 1868, p. 300.
[6] White *versus* Clements, Georgia Reports, vol. 39, p. 232.

Such were the legal aspects of the question, which were of course less important than the political and the emotional aspects. The legislature passed upon the issue in the early part of September, 1868, by declaring all the colored members ineligible, and admitting to the vacated seats the candidates who had received respectively the next highest number of votes.[1] If there was some legal ground for unseating the negroes, there was none for seating the minority candidates. It was done on the authority of the clause in Irwin's Code which said:

If at any popular election to fill any office the person elected is ineligible, . . . the person having the next highest number of votes, who is eligible, whenever a plurality elects, shall be declared elected.[2]

But this clause is found under the title "Of the Executive Department," and under the sub-head "Regulations as to All Executive Offices and Officers." Under the next title "Of the Legislative Department," there is no such provision.

For a legislature to unseat some of the elected members because on not untenable legal grounds it finds them ineligible, is not unusual. But the act of the Georgia legislature could not, under the circumstances, be regarded in the ordinary way. It showed strong racial prejudice. It was a startling breach of the system which reconstruction had been designed to institute, committed the very moment after the federal government withdrew its hand. It fixed on Georgia at once the earnest and unfavorable attention of northern public opinion. This fact enabled the Georgia Republicans to bring the federal government again to their assistance.

Their leader, Governor Bullock, at the next session of Congress (December, 1868), presented a letter to the Senate, saying that Georgia had not yet been admitted to the Union.

[1] H. J., 1868, pp. 242, 247. S. J., 1868, pp. 278, 280.
[2] Irwin's Code, 1868, § 121.

She had not been admitted by the Omnibus Act, for that act provided that she should be admitted when certain things had been done, and those things had not been done. By the Reconstruction Act of Juiy 19, 1867, all persons elected in Georgia were required to take the Test Oath. The members of the present legislature had never taken it. Therefore the action which that body had taken on July 21st, regarding the Fourteenth Amendment, was not a ratification by a legislature formed acording to the Reconstruction Acts; it was simply a ratification by a body which called itself the legislature. Hence the Omnibus Act had not yet gone into effect as to Georgia, and Georgia was not yet entitled to representation in Congress.[1]

If this argument was valid in the winter of 1868, it must also have been valid in the preceding summer. Yet in July Bullock had made no objection to being inaugurated as governor of Georgia, on the ground that Georgia had not become a state. He had not refused on that ground to issue on September 10th a commission to Joshua Hill, reciting that he had been regularly elected to the Senate of the United States by the legislature of the state, and signed " Rufus B. Bullock, governor." [2] The argument was an afterthought, not advanced until the expulsion of the negroes created a favorable opportunity for a hearing. It conflicted with the declarations and acts of the military authorities, and of the House of Representatives, but the sentiment aroused by the expulsion of the negroes was considered strong enough to sustain a repudiation of those declarations and acts.

Direct appeal to this sentiment was the auxiliary to the above argument. Bullock's letter to the Senate was accompanied by a memorial from a convention of colored men held at Macon in October. It said that there existed in Georgia

[1] C. G., 40th Congress, 3d session, p. 3.   [2] *Ibid.*, p. 2.

a spirit of hatred toward the negroes and their friends, which resulted in the persecution, political repression, terrorizing, outrage and murder of the negroes, in the burning of their schools, and in the slander, ostracism and abuse of their teachers and political friends. Of this the act of the legislature was an instance and an evidence. The aid of the federal government was implored.[1]

Similar charges had been made, it will be remembered, in the debates of 1866 and 1867. Now, however, they began to be urged with an earnestness and persistence altogether new. So conspicuous is this fact in the debates in Congress that a southern writer ironically remarks: "From this time forth the entire white race of the South devoted itself to the killing of negroes."[2] The rest of this chapter will be devoted to considering how much truth there was in the reported abuse of negroes and "loyal" persons.

We stated in Chapter II. that after the war a bitter jealousy and animosity toward the negroes arose among the lower class of the white population, and in Chapter IV. that the restless conduct of the negroes under the influences of reconstruction filled the upper class with such alarm that they formed secret organizations in self-defence. This practice, at first supported and led by good men of the higher class, simply for defence, soon fell into the hands of the poor white class, the criminal class, and the turbulent and discontented young men of all classes, and became an instrument of revenge, crime and oppression. The change, however, was not a complete transformation. A great deal of the whipping inflicted upon negroes was *bona fide* chastisement for actual misdemeanors. This mode of punishment was the natural product of the transition from the old social conditions, when the negroes were disciplined by their masters,

---

[1] C. G., 40th Congress, 3d session, p. 3.

[2] Richard Taylor, *Destruction and Reconstruction*.

to the new conditions.[1]   But besides these acts of correction many outrages were committed upon negroes,and also
upon white men, simply from malice or vengeance, or
other private motive.[2]   These outrages included some
homicides.[3]   The testimony of credible contemporaries be-
longing to both political parties agrees that the Ku Klux
Klan and similar organizations were used only to a very
small extent for political purposes.[4]

How many of these corrective or purely vicious acts were
perpetrated upon negroes?   Democrats of that time commonly said that the number was insignificant, that the peace
was as well kept in Georgia as in any northern state, and
that statements to the contrary were invented for political
purposes.[5]   The number was, indeed, greatly exaggerated
by Republicans, as some of the Republicans themselves
admitted.[6]   Making allowance for the warping of the truth
in both directions, and considering the statements of the
moderate Republicans,[7] and the admissions of some of the
Democrats,[8] remembering also the recent disbandment of the
army and the disturbed conditions of society, we must conclude that the attacks on negroes, made by disguised bands
and otherwise, were very numerous.

[1] K. K. R., vol. 6, p. 93 (testimony of Augustus R. Wright); p. 274 (testimony
of Ambrose R. Wright); p. 236 (testimony of J. H. Christy); p. 818 (testimony
of J. E. Brown).

[2] *Ibid*, vol. 7, pp. 812, 818 (testimony of J. E. Brown); p. 786 (testimony of B.
H. Hill).

[3] *Ibid.*, vol. 6, pp. 21 (testimony of C. D. Forsythe), 118 (testimony of Aug. R.
Wright); vol 7, pp. 988 (testimony of Linton Stephens), 1071.

[4] *Ibid.*, vol. 6, pp. 426, 440 (testimony of J. H. Caldwell), 108 (testimony of
Aug. R. Wright); vol. 7, p. 818 (testimony of J. E. Brown).

[5] *Ibid.*, vol. 6, p. 344 (testimony of J. B. Gordon).

[6] C. G., 41st Congress, 2d session, p. 1929 (Trumbull's remarks).

[7] Report of committee on reconstruction, H. M. D., 40th Congress, 3d session,
no. 52, pp. 12 (testimony of Akerman), 27 (testimony of J. E. Bryant).

[8] K. K. R., vol. 6, p. 107 (testimony of Aug. R. Wright).

The friends of the negroes also fared badly. Philanthropic women who came from the North to teach in the negro schools were almost invariably treated with contempt and avoided by the white people.[1] This was due partly to the lingering bitterness of the war and partly to the connection of the negro schools with the Freedmen's Bureau. This institution, the office of which was to set up strangers, from a recently hostile country, to instruct the southern people in their private affairs, was in itself odious. It was rendered more odious by the want of intelligence and tact, and even of honesty, which is said to have frequently characterized its officers. That the hatred thus aroused should be visited upon true philanthropists who were connected with the Bureau was unfortunate, but inevitable. As for the political friends of the negroes, the "loyal" men, or in other words the white men who supported reconstruction, they were habitually treated by the Conservative press and by Conservative speakers with violent invective. Conservative editors and orators neither engaged in nor recommended the slaughter or outrage of Radicals, but by continually voicing furious sentiments, they furnished encouragement to action of that sort by men of less intelligence and self-control.[2]

The accounts of lawlessness and persecution in Georgia, though exaggerated, undoubtedly had a substantial foundation. Whether this fact was a good argument for renewed interference in the state government by Congress is another question.

[1] K. K. R., vol. 7, p. 838 (testimony of C. W. Howard).

[2] This statement is corroborated by the testimony of B. H. Hill, K. K. R., vol. 7, p. 767.

CHAPTER VII

CONGRESSIONAL ACTION REGARDING GEORGIA FROM DECEMBER, 1868, TO DECEMBER, 1869.

ON December 7, 1868, the credentials of Joshua Hill, one of the Senators elected by the Georgia legislature in the previous July, were presented in the United States Senate. Immediately the letter of Governor Bullock and the memorial of the negro convention were also presented. These documents, seconded by a speech from a Senator dwelling on the fact that Georgia was under "rebel control," secured the reference of Hill's credentials to the committee on the judiciary.[1] This committee on January 25, 1869, recommended that Hill be not admitted to the Senate.[2]

The reason for this recommendation, said the committee's report, was that Georgia had failed to comply with the requirements of the Omnibus Act, and so was not yet entitled to representation in Congress. The failure here referred to was not that alleged by Bullock—that the members of the legislature had not taken the Test Oath—but the failure of the two houses to exclude persons disqualified by the Fourteenth Amendment. The Omnibus Act had provided that Georgia should be entitled to representation in Congress when her legislature had "*duly*" ratified the Fourteenth Amendment. The word *duly* meant *in a certain manner*— namely, the manner required by the rest of the act. The

---

[1] C. G., 40th Congress, 3d session, p. 2.

[2] S. R., 40th Congress, 3d session, no. 192.

failure to exclude the disqualified members was a departure from this manner.

We saw in Chapter V. that each of the committees appointed by the Georgia legislature in July to investigate the eligibility of members was divided, that both houses voted that all were eligible in the face of detailed evidence to the contrary, that the decision of the lower house contradicted the majority of its committee, and that Meade accepted the decision rather for the sake of convenience and finality than because it was indisputably correct. On these facts and on some independent investigation the Senate judiciary committee based its belief that the legislature had failed to obey the Omnibus Act in this respect.

Trumbull, of this committee, submitted a minority report. He admitted that the decision of the legislature may have been incorrect. But he protested that if the United States government intended to regard the presence of half a dozen ineligible members in a body of two hundred and nineteen as entirely vitiating the action of the legislature, it should have taken this stand at first. If at first it had, through its representative, Meade, overlooked the irregularity as a trifle, it seemed only just to continue to overlook it, and not to make it now the occasion for augmenting the turmoil in the state by fresh interference.

But the majority rejoined that there were very good reasons for not overlooking the irregularity. It was not a mere trifling departure from the letter of the act of Congress, it was a violation of the spirit of that act. "The obvious design" of the Omnibus Act " was to prevent the new organization from falling under the control of enemies of the United States." The expulsion of the negroes showed that that design had been frustrated and that the government was under " rebel control;" it showed a " common purpose to . . . resist the authority of the United States." Moreover, the "disorganized condition of society" in the state made it necessary for the federal government to intervene again in Georgia, not only to vindicate its law, but to preserve order.

The protest of Trumbull is significant as an early sign of the growth within the Republican party of an opposition to the prolongation of Congressional interference with the southern state governments.

The report of the judiciary committee was not acted upon, and thus the Senate avoided a categorical decision. But Hill was not admitted. A number of bills relating to Georgia were introduced; a bill "to carry out the Reconstruction Acts in Georgia" by Sumner,[1] a bill to repeal the act of June 25, 1868, in so far as it admitted Georgia, and to provide for a provisional government in that state, by Edmunds,[2] and others. All of these soon lapsed.

Meanwhile, in the House of Representatives the committee on reconstruction had been instructed to examine the public affairs of Georgia and to inquire what measures ought to be taken regarding the representatives of Georgia in the House.[3] Many citizens of Georgia, black and white, testified before the committee.[4] Among them Governor Bullock was conspicuous, advocating the enforcement of the Test Oath qualification—a fact which aroused great indignation in the state.

The doubtful position in which Georgia now hung raised the question, what should be done with her electoral votes in February, 1869? Congress had passed a joint resolution on July 20, 1868, to the effect that none of the states affected by the Omnibus Act should be entitled to vote in the Electoral College in 1869 unless at the time for choosing electors it had become entitled to representation in Con-

---

[1] C. G., 4cth Congress, 3d session, p. 27.   [2] *Ibid.*, p. 144.

[3] *Ibid.*, pp. 10 and 674.   [4] H. M. D., 40th Congress, 3d session, no. 52.

gress.[1]   As February 10, the day for counting the votes, approached, it was considered desirable, in order that the ceremony might pass off smoothly, that the Senate and the House should agree by a special rule what should be done with Georgia's votes.   Now, the Senate could not agree to a rule declaring that the votes should be counted, for that would imply that the state had become entitled to representation in Congress, and the Senate had refused to admit Hill.   But the House could not concur in declaring that the votes should not be counted; for that would imply that the state had not become entitled to representation in Congress, and the House had admitted seven Representatives from the state.   It was therefore agreed by a concurrent resolution passed February 8, that at the count of the electoral votes, in case the Georgia votes should be found not to affect the result essentially (which it was well known would be the case), then the presiding officer should make the following announcement:

Were the votes presented as of the state of Georgia to be counted, the result would be for ——— for President of the United States, — votes; if not counted, for ———, for President of the United States, — votes; but in either case ——— is elected President of the United States;

and a similar announcement of the votes for Vice-President.[2] Accordingly, on February 10, amid the wildest uproar, caused by the blunders of a perplexed chairman and the violent protest of a group of Representatives, led by Butler, against the execution of the special rule, which had been rushed through the House without their knowledge, it was announced that the electoral vote was as follows:

For Grant and Colfax
  Including Georgia's votes   .   .   214
  Excluding Georgia's votes   .   .   214

[1] U. S. L., vol. 15, Public Laws, p. 257.
[2] C. G., 40th Congress, 3d session, pp. 934, 976.   A precedent for this rule was found in the similar treatment of Missouri's electoral vote in 1821.

For Seymour and Blair
  Including Georgia's votes   .   .   80
  Excluding Georgia's votes   .   .   71

and that in either case Grant and Colfax were elected.[1]

On March 5, the first day of the forty-first Congress, the House of Representatives was able to get rid of the Georgia Representatives on a technicality. The same delegation which had represented Georgia since July, 1868, appeared again to finish its supposed term. Their credentials failed to state to what Congress they had been elected, but authorized them to take seats in the House of Representatives according to the ordinance of the Georgia constitutional convention passed March 10, 1868. Now, this ordinance provided that all the public officers who should be elected on April 20 should enter on their duties as soon as authorized by Congress or by the general commanding the military district, but should continue in the same as long as they would if elected in the November following.[2] These Congressmen, then, were elected to serve as if elected in November, 1868, that is, they were elected members of the forty-first Congress. But they had already served several months in the fortieth. If they should serve through the forty-first they would exceed the constitutional term. The convention of Georgia could make the first term of all state officers longer than the regular term subsequently to obtain; it could not so lengthen the term of members of the Congress of the United States. The credentials were referred to the committee of elections, and the House was thus relieved of the presence of the Georgia representatives, which would have been an embarrassment in the subsequent proceedings.[3]

[1] C. C. 40th Congress, 3d session, pp. 1057, ff.   [2] G. C., 1867-8, p. 567.

[3] C. G., 41st Congress, 1st session, pp. 16, 18. The committee of elections reported on Jan. 28, 1870, that the Georgia representatives were not entitled to seats in the 41st Congress, having sat in the 40th. R. C., 41st Congress, 2d session, no. 16.

Several bills relating to Georgia were then introduced, which, though they were not advanced very far, are worth noticing.[1] Their titles indicate the purpose "to enforce the Fourteenth Amendment." Now, the Fourteenth Amendment consists principally of prohibitions on states; it could not be enforced in Georgia unless Georgia was a state. Georgia had (it was assumed) admitted to her legislature men subject to the disqualifications of the Fourteenth Amendment, and had excluded men from the legislature on the ground of color, thus denying the equal protection of the laws to citizens. The latter act had been done after the Fourteenth Amendment went into effect (July 28, 1868[2]), the former before, but its effect continued. If Georgia was a state, then, she had violated the amendment, and Congress might correct these two acts by virtue of its power to enforce the amendment. If Georgia was not a state, she had not violated the Fourteenth Amendment, but her acts were subject to correction by Congress, because her government was "provisional only." If, therefore, Congress proposed to enforce the Fourteenth Amendment in Georgia, it acknowledged that Georgia was a state, and so debarred itself from any interference not necessary to enforce that Amendment. If it proposed to interfere simply as with a provisional government, there was no such limitation.

The bills of the first session of the forty-first Congress proposed to enforce the Fourteenth Amendment. To secure the enforcement of the disqualification clause they provided that each member of the legislature should be required to take an oath saying that he was not disqualified by the amendment, and that those who did not so swear should be excluded. To secure equal rights to the colored legislators they provided that all persons elected to the legislature (ac-

[1] C. G., 41st Congress, 1st session, pp. 8, 263, 591.

[2] U. S. L., vol. 15, appendix, p. xii.

cording to General Meade's announcement of the result of the election of 1868) who should take the test oath required should be admitted, and that the expulsion of the negroes should be declared void. The federal military authority was to assist in executing these measures if requested by the governor. These measures, it will be observed, were only such as might legally be taken regarding Massachusetts if it violated the Fourteenth Amendment.

At the next session of Congress, beginning in December, 1869, the policy of enforcing the Fourteenth Amendment was abandoned for the alternative policy of legislating for a provisional government. The reason for the change was an emergency in which the Republican Politicians found themselves. In the previous February Congress had passed the joint resolution proposing the Fifteenth Amendment. By December it seemed certain that the number of ratifying states would fall short of the required three-fourths by just one, unless Congress could prevent it.[1] Georgia furnished the means of preventing it. In March her legislature had rejected the proposed amendment.[2] It could now be forced to ratify and thus complete the necessary majority. Georgia must then be treated not as a state which had violated the Fourteenth Amendment, but as a provisional organization subject to the uncontrolled will of Congress. A bill was accordingly prepared containing the same provisions as the bills of the preceding session, but adding this clause: "That the legislature shall ratify the Fifteenth Amendment before Senators and Representatives from Georgia are admitted to seats in Congress." In accordance with its different legal basis the bill was entitled: "An act to promote the reconstruction of the state of Georgia."

Little need be said of the manner in which this bill was

[1] W. A. Dunning, *The Civil War and Reconstruction*, pp. 226–228, 243.
[2] S. J., 1869, p. 806; H. J., p. 610.

passed. The usual partisan abuse prevailed on both sides.
The Democrats made a remarkable opposition, led by Beck
of Kentucky.[1] The Republicans were aided by a message
from President Grant urging the intervention of Congress,[2]
by the report of the reconstruction committee on affairs in
Georgia,[3] and by a report from General Terry, who was
stationed in the Department of the South, alleging that
disorder was rampant in Georgia and the need of further military government by federal authority imperative.[4] Terry's
superior officer, General Halleck, added a postscript to
Terry's report to the effect that Terry was mistaken, that the
disorder in Georgia was much less than was commonly believed, and that federal interference was highly inadvisable.[5]
Aided by the report and undeterred by the postscript, the
Republicans discoursed of "rebel control" and "murder"
with unprecedented effect. Butler said that Congress must
act instantly; if action on the bill is postponed, he said, "the
rest of the Republican majority of that state may be
murdered, even during Christmas week, when the Son of
God came on earth to bring peace and good will to man."[6]

The bill became law on December 22, 1869.[7] Congress
thus decided at last to adopt the opinion of the Senate judiciary committee, that Georgia had not become a state
through the Omnibus Act. General Meade, in declaring the
contrary, had been mistaken. Bullock, in calling himself
governor, had been mistaken. The House of Representatives, in admitting members sent from Georgia, had been

---

[1] C. G., 41st Congress, 2d session, p. 251.   [2] *Ibid.*, p. 4.

[3] H. M. D., 40th Congress, 3d session, no. 52.

[4] S. D., 41st Congress, 2d session, no. 3.

[5] *Ibid.* Halleck's annual report of Nov. 6, 1869, speaks to the same effect.
R. S. W., 1869, abridged edition, p. 70.

[6] C. G., 41st Congress, 2d session, p. 246.

[7] U. S. L., vol. 16, Pub. Laws, p. 59.

mistaken; they were *de facto* members, but had no legal right there.[1]   The legal basis of the act of December 22 was then the same as that of the original Reconstruction Acts.

The question which had been raised in the debates on these acts—What legal effect could the action of a body not the legislature of a state have on the adoption of an amendment to the constitution?—was raised again here.   Some of the Republicans argued that such action could have no effect and should not be required.[2]   Under these circumstances there was a more earnest effort than any heretofore made to defend such a requirement.   It was answered: True, the body which will ratify the amendment in Georgia will not be a state legislature at the time; but it will later become a state legislature, and then by relation the ratification will be imputed to the state legislature and will thus have legal effect. Relation, an operation known to private law, had been applied to constitutional law in several previous cases, in order to give to acts done by the legislatures of territories the same effect as if they had been done after statehood was obtained.[3]   The ratification by Georgia would be valid by relation.[4]

[1] C. G., 41st Congress, 2d session, p. 1710 (Lawrence's speech).

[2] *Ibid.*. pp. 165 (Carpenter's speech) and 208 (Conkling's speech).

[3] C. G., 41st Congress, 2d session, p. 2062.

[4] *Ibid.*, p. 1710 (Lawrence's speech).

CHAPTER VIII

THE EXECUTION OF THE ACT OF DECEMBER 22, 1869, AND THE FINAL RESTORATION

BEFORE relating the manner in which the act of December 22, 1869 (which we shall call the Reorganization Act), was executed, we must mention its provisions in more detail than we did in the last chapter. It first "authorized and directed" the governor by proclamation to summon "forthwith" all persons elected to the legislature in April, 1868, according to Meade's announcement of the result of the election then held,[1] to meet in special session "on some day certain." The act continued:

and thereupon the said general assembly shall proceed to perfect its organization in conformity with the Constitution and laws of the United States, according to the provisions of this act.

When the legislature was assembled, every person claiming to be a member should take a test oath prescribed in the act, to the effect that he had never been a member of Congress or of a state legislature, nor held any civil office created by law for the administration of any general law of a state, or for the administration of justice in any state, or under the laws of the United States, nor served in the military or naval forces of the United States as an officer, and thereafter engaged in or supported hostilities against the United States; each person should take this oath or else an oath (also prescribed *verbatim*) that he had been relieved from disability by Congress according to section 3 of the

[1] G. O. T. M. D., 1868, no. 90.

Fourteenth Amendment. The exclusion on the ground of color of any person elected and otherwise qualified, the act declared " would be illegal and revolutionary," and was " prohibited." The act directed the President to use force in executing the act upon application from the governor.

The process ordered by the act seems simple and obvious, but the general of the army deduced much from it not apparent on its face. This act, he reasoned, implies that the Georgia government is provisional, and has never ceased to be so since March 2, 1867. And in that case the act of March 2, 1867, has never ceased to operate as to Georgia, since by its own terms it is to remain in force in each " rebel state " until each respectively has been " by law admitted to representation in the congress of the United States." Georgia has not been so admitted, since she did not comply with the Omnibus Act. Therefore the Reconstruction Acts are still in force in Georgia, and the general orders of July 28, 1868, declaring the Third Military District abolished were a mistake. Accordingly those orders were countermanded by the general of the army on January 4, 1870, and General Terry, a prominent advocate, as we have seen, of the revival of military government in Georgia, was placed in command of the remnant of the Third Military District.[1]

The War Department's deduction from the Reorganization Act of authority to institute again the system of the Reconstruction Acts came a month or two later under the consideration of the Senate judiciary committee, and was pronounced a gratuitous perversion of the act last passed. That act implied, to be sure, that the Georgia government was provisional; but it was plainly intended not to revive but to supersede the former regulations regarding that government. The purpose of the Reorganization Act was simply that the

[1] G. O. II., 1870, no. 1. This and other documents relating to Terry's administration are published in E. D., 41st Congress, 2d session, no. 288.

legislature should reorganize itself and ratify the Fifteenth Amendment. To this purpose military government had no relation. The Reconstruction Acts had not expired according to their own provisions as to Georgia, it was true, but they had been repealed by the Reorganization Act. This was further proved by the latter's provision that military force should be used " upon the application of the governor." The Reorganization Act, said the committee, "invokes military action in what it provides shall be done, and no more."[1] Unfortunately this opinion was delivered some time after the theory which it demolished had been in practical operation.

Terry, having received the *rôle* of military governor, played it as the true heir to the power of his great predecessors. He removed from office three sheriffs and a county ordinary and appointed successors.[2] He intervened in eight private controversies and composed them with a strong hand.[3] In two cases before the state courts he substituted his command for the regular process.[4] Still more apparent was the official character which he had assumed, in his conduct toward the legislature. Possessing the power wielded by Pope and Meade, he could issue any orders he pleased to that body. For this reason, and because he was in sympathy with them, the Georgia Republicans ardently embraced and tenaciously clung to the theory that he was not a mere assistant in executing the Reorganization Act, but a military governor under the Reconstruction Acts.

On December 22, 1869, Governor Bullock issued his proclamation (which he signed " Rufus B. Bullock, Provisional Governor "), summoning the men elected to the legislature in 1868 to meet in Atlanta on January 10 following.[5] This

[1] S. R., 41st Congress, 2d session, no. 58.

[2] G. O. M. D. G., 1870, no. 2, 14, 16, 17.

[3] S. O. M. D. G., no. 4, 5, 6, 8, 9, 11, 14, 17.   [4] *Ibid.*, no. 10 and 11.

[5] H. J., 1870, p. 3.

duty, besides that of calling on the President for aid if he saw fit, was the only one expressly entrusted to Bullock by the Reorganization Act. Another one, however, was deduced by the following process of reasoning: The legislature can do nothing before its members are qualified according to the act. Since it can do nothing, it cannot even organize itself. But it is the purpose of the act that the legislature be organized. Therefore some one else must be intended to organize it. This duty naturally belongs to the governor, since the cognate duty of convening the body is imposed on him. In accordance with this reasoning, Bullock appointed a temporary clerk for each house, who should call the house to order and preside until all the members should be qualified or declared disqualified, by taking or failing to take one of the test oaths of the Reorganization Act.[1] This appointment of Bullock rested not only upon the reasoning stated above, but upon the approval of Terry, who, whether the reasoning was correct or not, could do, or order to be done, to the legislature anything he chose.[2]

When the legislature convened on January 10, each house was called to order by its temporary clerk, who proceeded to call the roll of names announced by Meade after the election of 1868, for the administration to each person of one of the required test oaths. On the same day the upper house completed the roll call and the swearing in of members, and effected a permanent organization. A Republican (Conley) was elected president by a large majority. On assuming the chair he delivered an oration, the spirit of which may be perceived from the following sentence: "The government has determined that in this republic, which is not, never was, and never can be, a democracy—that in this republic Republicans shall rule."[3]

[1] S. J., 1870, p. 3; H. J., p. 7.   [2] H. J., p. 17.
[3] S. J., 1870., p. 26.

Far different was the course of events in the lower house. When that house assembled it found one Harris in the chair. Forgetting that his appointment had been indorsed by Terry and that he was, therefore, the virtual agent of a military governor who had the power to do anything he chose to the legislature, the Conservatives raised objection to his presiding and attempted to elect a temporary chairman in the usual way. This attempt precipitated a violent scene in the house, but was unsuccessful. Harris kept his seat and ordered the roll call for the swearing in of members to proceed. The names of seventy-eight persons were called and as many of these as were present were sworn in. At this point, the journal records, "the clerk *pro tem.* announced that the house would take a recess" until the next day. This the house did.[1] On January 11 and 12, the same proceedings occurred, the swearing in continuing until it was suspended and the house adjourned by the "clerk *pro tem.*"[2]

Without the theory that the Reconstruction Acts were still in force these proceedings in the lower house would have constituted the plainest illegality. But if Terry was a military governor and Harris his agent, they were legal. Though the Senate judiciary committee later declared this a false interpretation of the law, yet it was the official interpretation of the War Department, as we saw by the order appointing Terry.[3] The War Department had a right to decide what the Reorganization Act, which it was to aid in executing, meant. Its decision, whatever its character, was never officially overruled. Therefore the proceedings in the legislature were officially regular.

Before the legislature met, the Conservative papers had published an article by a state judge on the meaning of the first test oath of the Reorganization Act. It concerned

---

[1] H. J., 1870, p. 3.   [2] *Ibid.*, pp. 19 and 21.
[3] See also a letter from Sherman to Terry, published in K. K. R., vol. i, p. 311.

especially the phrase: "any civil office created by law for the administration of any general law of a state." It was argued that there were many state offices not included in this phrase—among them those of mayor, alderman and state librarian. Since these offices were not "for the administration of any general law," but only for that of special or local law, former occupants of them who had supported the Confederacy could take the present test oath.[1] This construction would give an advantage to the Conservatives. To counteract it, Bullock applied to the attorney general for an official interpretation. That officer (Farrow by name) responded with a very reasonable opinion. He admitted that officers with merely local functions were not included in the phrase in question, but pointed out that many municipal officers had the powers of a justice of the peace. In such cases they were charged with the administration of general law and were included in the phrase. The state librarian, said Farrow, executed general law and was included.[2]

After the swearing in of members had gone on in the house of representatives, as we have said, it was believed by the Radicals that some Conservatives were acting upon the judge's interpretation and disregarding the attorney general's, and that others had sworn or intended to swear falsely who were debarred even by the former. Ordinarily, if a man intends to swear falsely to a test oath there is no way of preventing him. In the existing state of public opinion, prosecution for perjury after the oath of office was taken was impossible. But Georgia had a military governor. By issuing orders he could prevent men whom he believed ineligible from swearing and could unseat those whom he believed to have sworn falsely. This Terry decided to do.

On January 13 he detailed a board of soldiers to investigate the cases of twenty-one members elect whose eligibility

---

[1] Judge Cabaniss in Atlanta *Constitution*, Jan. 8, 1870.   [2] H. J., 1870, p. 9.

was questioned.[1] This board sat for two weeks, and found
five men ineligible[2] and eleven eligible.[3] Terry accordingly
forbade the five, and ordered the eleven, to be sworn in. The
remaining five of the twenty-one, together with nineteen
others, confessed ineligibility by filing with Bullock application for the removal of their disabilities by Congress. These
also Terry forbade to be sworn in.[4] The actions and the decision of the board of inquiry were pronounced fair and honorable even by the Conservatives.[5] The nineteen applica-
tions for Congressional grace were said to have been pro-
cured by the Radicals through intimidation and fraud.[6] If
the applicants were in fact ineligible but intended nevertheless
to take the oath, then we must admire the cleverness of the
Radicals in dissuading them, by whatever means they did it.
If they used intimidation and fraud, their means were no
worse than the end sought by their victims—the frustration
of a law by perjury. On the other hand, if nineteen Conservatives who were eligible were induced by Radicals to peti-
tion for the removal of ineligibility, the fact may excite disapproval of the Radicals, but hardly pity for the Conservatives.

On January 13, when the board of inquiry was appointed,
the "clerk *pro tem.*" of the lower house, by order of Bullock
countersigned by Terry, had declared the house adjourned
till January 17, to await the decision of the board.[7] On the
17th the house met and listened to the reading of two orders
from Bullock indorsed by Terry; the one directing the state
treasurer to issue fifty dollars to each member of the house,

[1] G. O. M. D. G., 1870, no. 3 and 4.

[2] *Ibid.*, no. 9 and 11.   [3] *Ibid.*, no. 9.

[4] *Ibid.*, no. 9 and 11.   [5] Atlanta *Constitution*, Jan. 27, 1870.

[6] C. G., 41st Congress, 2d session, p. 1926 (Trumbull's speech).

[7] H. J., 1870, p. 22.

the other ordering the house to adjourn till January 19.[1]
On the 19th the house met, and after one man had been
sworn in was adjourned in the same manner till the 24th.[2]
On the 24th it met and after two men had been sworn in was
again adjourned by order of the governor.[3] On the morn-
ing of the 25th it met and was adjourned till afternoon. In
the afternoon it was adjourned as soon as it had met till the
next day. To the countersignature of Terry in this case was
added the promise that this was the last adjournment of the
series, since the board had now rendered so much of its decision as related to members of the lower house. The house
was therefore ordered to swear in, on the next day, all the
remaining members elect except those found or confessed
ineligible, and to elect its permanent officers.[4] On January
26 this order was complied with; the Radical candidate for
chairman was elected by a large majority, and the redoubt-
able "clerk *pro tem.*," having presided for the last time,
retired.[5]

The reorganized legislature on February 2 complied with
the remaining requirements of the Reorganization Act by
ratifying the Fifteenth Amendment. On the advice of Bullock it also repassed the resolutions of July, 1868, required
by the Omnibus Act. This was not necessary to re-admis-
sion. It is true, the requirements of the Omnibus Act had,
by the hypothesis of the Reorganization Act, never been
"duly" fulfilled. But the Omnibus Act had been super-
seded by other legislation, which made new requirements
and did not renew the old. The renewal of the unfulfilled
requirements had been discussed in Congress and rejected.[6]
Nevertheless, the resolutions were passed gratuitously.[7]

The Omnibus Act had definitely said that Georgia should

[1] H. J., 1870, p. 23.   [2] *Ibid.*, p. 25.   [3] *Ibid.*, p. 26.
[4] G. O. M. D. G., 1870, no. 10.   [5] H. J., 1870, p. 33.
[6] C. G., 41st Congress, 2d session, p. 208.   [7] S. J., 1870, p. 74; H. J., p. 74.

be "entitled and admitted to representation in Congress as a state of the union when the legislature" had complied with the conditions mentioned in the act. The Reorganization Act was not so definite. It said; "The legislature shall ratify the Fifteenth Amendment . . . before Senators and Representatives from Georgia are admitted to seats in Congress." This might be construed as granting title to representation as a state as soon as the Fifteenth Amendment should be ratified, or as merely requiring the ratification and making no definite provision as to restoration but leaving that subject to be provided for by another act. The latter construction was adopted by the Georgia Radicals, since it prolonged the tenure of their military governor. It followed from this construction that the state government was still "provisional" and could not proceed with its business like a regular state government. So after electing United States Senators (the election of July, 1868, being regarded as invalid,[1] and the present election probably being designed to become valid by relation), the legislature adjourned until April 18, to await Congressional action.[2] In April Congress had taken no action, and the legislature, after sitting a fortnight, took another recess of two months.[3] Meantime the theory of military government had been faithfully observed. Though the legislature was only provisional, it could legislate with Terry's permission. It passed a stay law on February 17, and asked Terry to enforce it.[4] On May 2 it passed revenue and appropriation acts,[5] but not before Terry had informed it through the governor that he would allow those acts to have the validity of regularly issued military orders.[6]

Whatever may have been the merits of the construction of

---

[1] See Bullock's message, H. J., 1870, p. 52.

[2] H. J., 1870, p. 95.   [3] *Ibid.*, pp. 113, 156.

[4] H. J., 1870, p. 106.   [5] *Ibid.*, p. 140.   [6] *Ibid.*, p. 121.

the Reorganization Act adopted by the War Department, it
is certain that the proceedings taken under it greatly aston-
ished those who had passed the act. On January 19 the
House of Representatives adopted a resolution requesting
the general of the army to inform it by what authority three
United States soldiers were acting as a committee in the
legislature of Georgia.[1] On February 4 the Senate asked
for official information regarding the proceedings had under
the Reorganization Act.[2] The facts disclosed in response to
this request created such surprise that the Senate directed
the judiciary committee to inquire and report whether the
act had been complied with.[3] The answer of the committee,
as we saw in the early part of the chapter, was that the act
had been misconstrued and violated. The appointment of
presiding officers by the governor, the acts of those officers,
the revival of the military governorship, and in particular the
interference of Terry in the organization of the legislature—
these, said the committee, were wholly unlawful. But though
unlawful they had resulted in no substantial injustice, since
all the men debarred by Terry were undoubtedly ineligible.
And in any case a general state election was approaching,
so that if any injustice had been done it would soon be
righted. For these reasons the committee recommended
that Congress undertake no more legislation for Georgia, but
admit her representatives to each house as soon as possible.[4]

The committee believed that the Reorganization Act was
to be construed as a law entitling Georgia to representation
in Congress as soon as she had ratified the Fifteenth Amendment. This opinion was held by many Republicans, who
had followed Trumbull's example and who appeared from

[1] C. G., 41st Congress, 2d session, p. 576. For Sherman's reply see E. D., 41st
Congress, 2d session, no. 82.

[2] C. G., 41st Congress, 2d session, p. 1029.   [3] *Ibid.*, p. 1128.

[4] S. R., 41st Congress, 2d session, no. 58.

this time on as opponents of further Congressional interference in the South. The radical Republicans, however, led by Butler—those Republicans characterized by a Republican paper of the time as "the screeching wing" of the party [1]— insisted that Georgia must be admitted, as the first Reconstruction Act had said, "by law," and that no law to that effect had been passed. The reason why this argument was urged was that the passage of a new act for restoring the state would give an opportunity to annex other provisions besides the declaration of restoration. The particular provisions designed to be annexed were for the purpose of prolonging the term of the present state government.

On February 25 Butler introduced the bill to admit Georgia.[2] One of its sections was as follows:

> That the power granted by the constitution of Georgia to the general assembly to change the time of holding elections . . . shall not be so exercised as to postpone the election for members of the next general assembly beyond the Tuesday after the first Monday in November in the year 1872.

The power here referred to was that conferred by Article III., section 1, of the state constitution;

> The election for members of the general assembly shall begin on Tuesday after the first Monday in November of every second year . . . but the general assembly may by law change the time of election, and members shall hold until their successors are elected and qualified.

The constitutional term of the present legislature (except of one-half of the senators, who held four years) would expire in November, 1870. But this section of the constitution, Butler pointed out, would enable the legislature to postpone the election and perpetuate its power. This grave danger he proposed to remove by the clause of his bill above quoted. In order to prevent the legislature from prolonging its tenure forever, he proposed, not to forbid prolongation, but to allow it for two years.

[1] Chicago *Tribune*, Dec. 7, 1868.
[2] C. G., 41st Congress, 2d session, pp. 1570, 1704.

I also propose [he said] by this [clause] to give to the present State officers of Georgia a two years' term of office in that state as a state in this Union.

That Congress should pose as the defender of the people of Georgia against a usurping legislature, and at the same time by the guaranty of its approval encourage that legislature to double its constitutional term—this was a conception of political genius which, independently of its realization, should make Butler immortal.

The moderate Republicans of the House of Representatives were willing, for the sake of settling doubt, to pass a bill declaring Georgia restored, but were decidedly opposed the scheme to use the bill as a means of prolonging the tenure of the Georgia Radicals. An admendment to Butler's bill, known as the Bingham amendment, was offered, to the following effect:

. . . neither shall this act be construed to extend the official tenure of any officer of said state beyond the term limited by the constitution thereof, dating from the election or appointment of such officer.[1]

The bill with this amendment passed the House by a large majority on March 8.[2]

In the Senate the necessity of any bill and the propriety of the Bingham amendment were warmly debated for some weeks. Then the so-called Drake amendment was offered. It provided that whenever the legislature or governor of any state should inform the President of the existence within that state of associations organized for the purpose of obstructing the law and doing violence to persons, then the President should send troops to that state, declare martial law, suspend the privileges of the writ of *habeas corpus*, and take such other military measures as he saw fit, and should levy the cost of the expedition on the people of the state.[3] The propriety of grafting this general measure on a special bill like the present should not be discussed, it was said, in view of

---

[1] C. G., 41st Congress, 2d session, p. 1770.   [2] *Ibid.*   [3] *Ibid.*, p. 1988.

the pressing necessity of passing it in some way, no matter how.[1] The debate thus complicated continued until April 19, when the bill went to the committee of the whole. There, the night being far spent, two entirely new amendments were suddenly offered. One commanded Georgia to hold a general election in the present year; the other declared that the existing government of Georgia was still "provisional" and provided that the Reconstruction Acts of 1867 should continue to be enforced there. These amendments were adopted by the committee. The Drake amendment was also adopted. Finally, the entire bill as it came from the house was stricken out.[2] Thus transformed so that, as a Senator said, "it would not be recognized by the oldest inhabitant," the bill was passed by the Senate.[3]

The House of Representatives did not take up the bill again until June 23. On June 24 it decided to insist on the passage of the bill substantially as before passed.[4] As a result of the conference following, the Senate yielded to the House. The bill became law on July 15, 1870. It said:

. . . It is hereby declared that the state of Georgia is entitled to representation in the Congress of the United States. But nothing in this act contained shall be construed to deprive the people of Georgia of the right to an election for members of the general assembly of said state, as provided for in the constitution thereof.[5]

One would suppose that this act of July 15 should close the chapter; that it recognized Georgia as a state, and that henceforth all peculiar relations between Georgia and the federal government were at an end. The Georgia Radicals were able to avoid this conclusion. In a message to the legislature on July 18 the governor said that according to the act of March 2, 1867, the federal military power was to re-

---

[1] C. G., 41st Congress, 2d session, p. 2091.   [2] *Ibid.*, pp. 2820, ff.

[3] *Ibid.*, p. 2829.   [4] *Ibid.*, p. 4747.

[5] U. S. L., vol. 16, Public Laws, p. 363.

main until the state was not only entitled to representation but actually represented in Congress. Section 5 of that act contained this language:

When . . . any one of said rebel states shall have [fulfilled all requirements], said state shall be declared entitled to representation in Congress, and Senators and Representatives shall be admitted therefrom . . . and then and thereafter the preceding sections of this act shall be inoperative in said state.

Hence, the military authority, said Bullock, would continue in Georgia until the following December. But he informed the legislature that it might proceed with legislation, since Terry had informed him that he would allow it.[1]

The Radicals in the legislature took advantage of the theory announced by the governor to make one last attempt at prolongation of power. On July 26 a resolution was offered in the upper house to this effect: That the authority of the United States was still paramount in Georgia; that no offence ought to be offered to Congress by an apparent denial of this fact; that therefore no election should be held in the state until Congress had fully recognized its statehood by receiving its representatives.[2] On July 29 the senate adopted a resolution similar to this, but the lower house rejected it by a few votes.[3] With the failure of this attempt, the Reconstruction Acts ceased to operate in Georgia, either in fact or in any one's theory.

At the next session of Congress a delegation from Georgia composed of men elected in December, 1870, was seated in the House of Representatives.[4] In the Senate, Farrow and Whitely, elected by the legislature in February, 1870, presented credentials. They were referred to the judiciary committee, which reported adversely. It recommended that Hill, elected in 1868, be seated, and reported that Miller,

[1] H. J., 1870, p. 181.
[2] S. J., 1870, vol. ii, p. 29. [3] *Ibid.*, p. 50; H. J., p. 343.
[4] C. G., 41st Congress, 3d session, pp. 527, 530, 678, 703, 1086.

elected with Hill, would be entitled to a seat except that he was unable to take the Test Oath required of members of Congress by the act of July 2, 1862.[1]　Since this committee had decided in January, 1869, that the Georgia legislature was not legally organized in 1868, and in March, 1870, that its organization in January of that year was also illegal, and since therefore the election of Hill and Miller and that of Farrow and Whitely were both illegal, the committee had to decide the question: To which of these illegal elections ought we to give *de facto* validity?　It decided in favor of the earlier one on grounds of equity.　The Senate adopted the committee's opinion.　The Test Oath act was suspended in favor of Miller by a special act of Congress, and he and Hill were sworn in, in February, 1871.[2]

Thus, after federal intervention had been imposed in 1865 and apparently withdrawn in the same year, again imposed in 1867 and again apparently withdrawn in 1868, and yet again imposed in 1869, it was now withdrawn for the last time, and Georgia was completely restored to statehood.

[1] S. R., 41st Congress, 3d session, no. 308.

[2] C. G., 41st Congress, 3d session, pp. 871, 1632.

CHAPTER IX

RECONSTRUCTION AND THE STATE GOVERNMENT.

IN the preceding chapters we have mentioned the immediate effect of reconstruction upon social conditions. To its immediate effects upon political conditions, in other words to the character and conduct of the new state government, which have been mentioned only incidentally, we shall now give a more direct and consecutive consideration.

With reference to the political reforms of reconstruction the white men of Georgia formed three distinct parties. There were those who favored them, either on their ethical and political merits or (more often) as a means of attaining political power otherwise unattainable. They were called Scalawags, Carpet-baggers and Radicals, of which terms we we shall adopt the last. There were those unalterably opposed to them, called Rebels by their critics and Conservatives by themselves. There were, thirdly, those who supported them not upon their merits, which they doubted, but because they saw the state at the mercy of a conqueror and believed that, bad as the measures were, it was better to accept them quickly than to make a vain resistance, which could only prolong the social and commercial disturbances in the state, and which might occasion the administration of a still worse dose. This group embraced many of the commercial class, which was especially large in Georgia, and one of the men prominent in former politics, namely Governor Brown. They were classed by the Conservatives with the basest of Radicals, but we shall call them the Moderate Republicans. The admixture of this group with the Radical

party had important consequences. Differing from their party
in principle and allying themselves with it to bring peace to
the state, when the peace of the state seemed secure, they
sometimes adhered to their principles rather than to their
party. It is true, many of them became so interested in the
great game of politics then going on that they played it for
its own sake; but some party splits of importance occurred.

The first fruit of the policy of negro enfranchisement and
rebel disenfranchisement was the constitutional convention of
1867–68. It was stated in the latter part of Chapter IV. that
in the election for members of this convention many Conservatives declined to take part. For this reason the Radicals
obtained a predominance in the convention which they did
not retain in the state government after the Conservatives
decided to fight. The convention, in fact, was extremely
Radical. The constitution which it framed shows the thor-
oughness with which it entered into the Humanitarian reforms.
The speeches and resolutions show that a close sympathy
with the Republican party and a bitter antagonism to the
Conservatives were entertained by most of the members.
The temporary chairman, Foster Blodgett, in his opening
speech, mentioned the suspicious, hostile and contemptuous
attitude of the Conservatives toward the convention. He said:

They may stand and rail at us and strive to distract us from our patriotic labors;
but we are engaged in a great work . . . we are building up the walls of a
great state.[1]

Parrot, the permanent chairman, said:

Many of us come here from amongst a people who have spurned us and spit
upon us . . . the enemies of the convention are watching with envious eyes
to see whether we shall be able to meet public expectation . . . We should
form a state government for an unwilling people based upon the soundest principles . . . and in governing them rescue human liberty from the grave, and
prevent them from trampling us under foot.

On the other side, he said:

[1] J. C., p. 14.

The Republican party of the nation is waiting with intense anxiety the move-
ments of this body. Our friends will soon be able to determine whether we shall
be a burden upon them . . . or aid them in the great work of restoring our
state.[1]

When Governor Jenkins brought suit against Stanton on
behalf of the state, the convention declared the action un-
authorized and in the name of the people of Georgia de-
manded that the suit be dismissed.[2] On December 17, 1867,
a resolution was passed, asking Pope to appoint, in lieu of
Governor Jenkins, a provisional governor, and asking that
the person appointed be Rufus B. Bullock.[3] Unsuccessful
here, the convention tried again on January 21. It requested
Congress to allow it to vacate the governorship and all other
offices now filled by men unfriendly to reconstruction and to
fill them with new appointees.[4] These two last named resolutions suggest not only Radical sentiment, but also Radical
organization in the convention.

The attitude of the convention toward the military authorities was most cordial. On December 20, a reception was
given to Pope. The general made a speech and received an
ovation.[5] Resolutions of friendship and gratitude were voted
him on his departure.[6] Meade, on his arrival, received resolutions of welcome,[7] and resolutions of friendly import on
various other occasions.[8] Meade did not entirely reciprocate
this cordiality.

Toward Congress the convention was not only cordial; it
was almost filial. Not only was the United States government eloquently thanked for its magnanimity,[9] but it was
appealed to by the convention as a kind parent by a child
confident of favor. It was petitioned to appropriate thirty
million dollars to be loaned on mortgage to southern

---

[1] J. C., pp. 16, 17.

[2] *Ibid.*, p. 587.

[3] *Ibid.*, pp. 49, 53

[4] *Ibid.*, p. 581.

[5] *Ibid.*, p. 75.

[6] *Ibid.*, p. 63.

[7] *Ibid.*, p. 84.

[8] *Ibid.*, pp. 581, 594.

[9] *Ibid.*, p. 68.

planters;[1] to loan a hundred thousand dollars to the South Georgia and Florida railroad,[2] and "to make a liberal appropriation" for building the proposed Air Line railroad.[3]

The constitutional convention of 1865 had met on October 25, and adjourned on November 8, thus completing its work in fourteen days. This dispatch, as well as the style of its resolutions and of the speeches of its members,[4] had marked it as a body where good taste, decorum and public spirit prevailed.

The reconstruction convention met on December 9, 1867, and continued in session (excepting a recess from December 24 to January 7), until March 11, 1868. The first article of the new constitution on which the convention took action was reported on January 9.[5] Before that time many resolutions and ordinances were introduced. Most of them related to "relief" (such as suspension of tax collections, homestead exemption, stay of execution for debt, etc.), or to the pay and mileage of delegates, and only rarely was anything said about the constitution. On December 16 the more conscientious members secured the appointment of a committee to inquire whether the convention had power to do any business besides frame a constitution.[6] This committee did not discuss the law of the question, but recommended on moral grounds a resolution to this effect:

That all ordinances or other matter . . . already introduced and pending are hereby indefinitely postponed; and in future no ordinance or other matter . . . not necessarily connected with the fundamental law shall be entertained by this convention [except relief legislation].

This report met with vigorous opposition. It was saved from the table by two votes. But it was adopted.[7] The

---

[1] J. C., p. 583.   [2] *Ibid.*, p. 593.   [3] *Ibid.*, p. 591.
[4] See J. C., 1865, p. 201 (speech of H. V. Johnson).
[5] .C., 1867–8, p. 90.   [6] *Ibid.*, p. 39.   *Ibid.*, p. 47.

contemporary Conservative press describes the convention as very infamous and very disgusting.[1] It contained thirty-three negroes, and the transactions recorded in the official journal show that it was composed largely of men of low character.

Hence, to many of the delegates, framing the constitution was only a minor incident of the convention, and the main part of that work was left to a small number of men. Their work shows intelligence and ability. Moreover, in the records of the convention there are not wanting traces of that undoubted public spirit which animated many of the supporters of reconstructien—the honest desire to repair and develop the material welfare of the state. This spirit is evident in the speeches we have cited, and in some of the resolutions.

We have stated how the campaign of 1868 resulted in giving the governorship to the Republicans and a majority of twenty-nine in the legislature to the Conservatives; how Governor Bullock tried to reduce that majority through Meade, and how Meade refused his aid; and how the majority was more than doubled by the expulsion of the negroes and the seating of the minority candidates. From that time to the reorganization of the legislature in 1870, the most remarkable fact in the state politics was the hostility between the governor and the legislature.

After the expulsion of the negroes, the lower house asked the governor to send it the names of the candidates who at the election had received the next highest vote to the persons expelled. The governor sent the names and with them a long protest against the expulsion of the negroes.[2] The house, on hearing the message, adopted a tart resolution, reminding the governor that the members of each house

---

[1] M. F. U., Dec. 24, 1867, Jan. 7, Jan. 14, 1868.

[2] H. J., 1868, p. 294.

were "the keepers of their own consciences, and not his Excellency." [1]   A similar message to the upper house in response to a similar request provoked a similar resolution, which was defeated by two votes. [2]

It will be remembered that in December, 1868, and January, 1869, the governor urged upon Congress, through his letter presented in the Senate and through his testimony before the Reconstruction Committee, the theory that Georgia had not yet been restored.   On January 15, 1869, he urged the same view upon the legislature.   He advised it to reorganize itself by summoning all men elected members in 1868, requiring each to take the Test Oath, excluding only those who should not take it, and thus constituted to repass the resolutions required by the Omnibus Act.   If the legislature did not do this, it must submit to Congressional interference. [3]   This message apparently caused the legislature some apprehension.   It adopted a joint resolution to the effect that it desired the question of the eligibility of negroes to office to be determined by the supreme court of the state.   The governor sent this resolution back with one of his admirably keen and powerful messages.   He said that Congress had two grievances against the present legislature; that it had admitted members disqualified by the Fourteenth Amendment, contrary to the Omnibus Act, and that it had expelled twenty-eight negroes.   The present resolution, intended to appease Congress, ignored the first grievance and proposed no remedy for the second; therefore it was meaningless and absurd. [4]

On January 21, 1869, the state treasurer, Angier, in response to an inquiry from the house of representatives regarding the affairs of his department, intimated that the governor had drawn money from the treasury under suspi-

[1] H. J., 1868, p. 303.   [2] S. J., 1868, p. 326.
[3] H. J., 1869, p. 5.   [4] *Ibid.*, p. 228.

cious circumsances.[1]   Thus began the feud between the governor and the treasurer which continued during the rest of Bullock's term.   Angier's report was referred to the committee on finance.   The majority of the committee reported that the governor's acts had been irregular but in good faith. The minority reported that his acts were culpable and his explanations inadequate, and concluded: "The facts herein set forth develop the necessity for further legislation for the security of the treasury."[2] This report the house adopted by a large majority.[3]

Another index of the relations between the governor and the legislature is furnished by the governor's message submitting the proposed Fifteenth Amendment.   It opened thus:

It is especially gratifying to learn, as I do from the published proceedings of your honorable body, that senators and representatives who have heretofore acted with a political organization which adopted as one of its principles a denunciation of the acts of a Republican Congress . . . should now give expression to their anxious desire to lose no time in embracing this opportunity of ratifying one of the fundamental principles of the Republican party . . . and I very much regret that the preparation necessary for a proper presentation of this subject to your honorable body has necessarily caused a short delay, and thereby prolonged the suspense of those who are so anxious to concur.[4]

The radicals probably desired the rejection of the amendment, since it would furnish another strong argument to Congress in favor of reorganizing the legislature.   Hence, the Radical governor, as his message shows, did not do his best to induce the legislature to ratify, and probably some Radical members for the same reason voted against the amendment or refrained from voting for it.   It was defeated in the lower house on March 12,[5] and in the upper on March 18.[6]

In the last chapter we saw that Terry excluded five men

---

[1] H. J., p. 54.   [2] *Ibid.*, p. 260.   [3] *Ibid.*, p. 265.
[4] H. J., 1869, p. 575.   [5] *Ibid.*, 1869, p. 618.   [6] S. J., p. 806.

from the legislature because the board of inquiry had found them ineligible, and excluded nineteen others because they had failed to take the required oath, and had applied to Congress for removal of disabilities. It is safe to assume that all of these twenty-four men were conservatives. Nineteen of them had been elected to the lower house, five to the senate.[1] Immediately after organization, on advice of Bullock and with the sanction of Terry, the senate gave the five vacated seats to the minority candidates,[2] and the house gave fourteen of its vacated seats to the minority candidates.[3] The result was that the Republicans secured a majority in each house.[4] The Republican control thus secured remained

[1] G. O. M. D. G., 1870, no. 9 and 11.

[2] S. J., 1870, p. 39.   [3] H. J., pp. 34, 40, 84, 88.

[4] The complexion of the legislature when composed of the men elected in April, 1868, was as follows:

	Senate.	Lower House.
Republicans.	22	73
Conservatives	22	102

After the colored members were expelled and their seats given to the minority candidates, it was as follows:

	Senate.	Lower House.
Republicans	19	48
Conservatives	25	127

After the reorganization of 1870 it was as follows:

	Senate.	Lower House.
Republicans	27	87
Conservatives	17	83

The figures in the second and third tables are based upon the changes produced

uninterrupted for the remainder of 1870.   Perfect accord now existed between the governor and legislature, and in the quarrel between Bullock and Angier, which went on with increased acerbity in the press and before a congressional committee,[1] the legislature proceeded to transfer its support to the governor.[2]

But Republican supremacy was in danger.   It was threatened by the Moderate Republicans.   J. E. Bryant, a Republican, prominent in the state politics since the beginning of the new *régime*, in testifying before the Reconstruction Committee in January, 1869, had advocated reorganization of the legislature, but had opposed any other interference, especially the restoration of military government.[3]   He and other Republicans who shared his opinion were disgusted with the proceedings of Bullock and Terry.   As early as January 12, 1870, there were reports that the Radicals were apprehensive of a combination between the Moderate Republicans and the Conservatives.[4]   Probably the strenuous efforts of the Radicals to take and make every possible advantage for themselves in the reorganization is partly accounted for by this apprehension.   On February 2, Bryant caused to be entered on the journal of the house of representatives a protest denouncing the reorganization proceedings as illegal.[5]   Shortly afterwards he published a statement of his position. He said that he was a Republican, but was opposed to the corrupt ring which controlled the party in Georgia.[6]   From

only by the official transactions referred to.   Perhaps some slight corrections might be made on account of accidental circumstances, such as the non-attendance or death of a few members.

[1] See K. K. R., vol. 6, p. 149; vol. 7, p. 1062.

[2] H. J., 1870, p. 156.

[3] H. M. D., 40th Congress, 3d session, no. 52, p. 27.]

[4] Savannah *News*, Jan. 12, 1870.

[5] H. J., p. 50.   [6] M. F. U., Feb. 15, 1870

this time on the papers frequently referred to the alliance between the followers of Bryant and the Conservatives as the salvation of the state.[1]

The Radical majority was not quite strong enough to pass a resolution declaring that there should be no election in 1870, as was attempted in August of that year.[2]　But it was strong enough to pass an election law very favorable to the Radical party.　It changed the date of the election from the regular time in November to December 22, and following the example set by General Pope in 1867, provided that it should continue three days.　It established a board of five election managers for each county, three to be appointed by the governor and senate, and two by the county ordinary. It provided that the board should have "no power to refuse the ballot of any male person of apparent full age, a resident of the county, who [had] not previously voted at the said election." Also it said: "They [the managers] shall not permit any person to challenge any vote."[3]　Another act was passed, calculated to prevent the loss of Republican votes through disqualification of negroes for non-payment of taxes. It declared the poll tax levied in 1868, 1869 and 1870 illegal.[4]

At the election thus provided for were to be chosen a new legislature (except half of the senators, who held four years) and Congressmen.　To what extent the Republicans availed themselves of the advantages offered by the election law we do not know.　At any rate, the Conservatives obtained two-thirds of the seats in the legislature, and five of the seven seats in Congress.[5]

This result meant trouble for the governor, whose term ran to November, 1872.　His efforts to secure Congressional interference, his conduct in January, 1870, and the accusa-

---

[1] M. F. U., Jan. 25, 1870.　　　　　[2] H. J., p. 343.

[3] S. L., 1870, p. 62.　　[4] *Ibid.*, p. 431.　　[5] Tribune Almanac, 1871, p. 75.

tions of extravagance, corruption, and other crimes continually made by an intemperate press, had raised public indignation to a high point. It was certain that when the new legislature met it would investigate the charges, and it was hoped that the governor would be impeached.[1] The time of reckoning had been postponed, however, by the prudence of the outgoing legislature, which had provided that the next session of the legislature should begin, instead of in January, the regular time set by the constitution,[2] on the first Wednesday in November, 1871.[3]

The first Wednesday in November, 1871, was November 1. On October 23, the governor recorded in the executive minutes that he resigned his office, for " good and sufficient reasons," the resignation to take effect on October 30.[4] He then quietly left the state. The fact that he had resigned was kept secret until October 30.[5]

In case of a vacancy in the office of governor, the constitution directed the president of the senate to fill the office.[6] On October 30, therefore, Conley, the president of the senate at its last session, hastened to be sworn in as governor.[7] By resigning just before the meeting of the incoming Conservative legislature, Bullock had thus cleverly prolonged Republican power, while at the same time resigning. The question whether under the constitution the governor's office should not be filled by the president of the newly-organized senate, was raised by the papers.[8] But Conley was by common consent left in possession of the office. Though, as he said in his first message to the legislature,[9] " a staunch Re-

---

[1] M. F. U., March 14, 1871; Atlanta *Constitution*, Oct. 26 and 31, 1871.

[2] Art. iii, sect. i, § 3.   [3] S. L., 1870, p. 419.

[4] E. M., 1870–74, p. 197.   [5] See entry of the secretary of state, *ibid*.

[6] Art. iv, sect. i, § 4.   [7] E. M., 1870–74, p. 198.

[8] Atlanta *Constitution*, Nov. 3, 1871.   [9] S. J., 1871, p. 17.

publican," he was not personally unpopular.[1] Moreover, the legislature intended to furnish a successor very soon.

On November 22, a bill was passed ordering a special election for governor for the remainder of the unexpired term, to be held on the third Tuesday in December.[2] The authority for this act was found in the following provision of the constitution: "The general assembly shall have power to provide by law for filling unexpired terms by a special election."[3] Conley vetoed the bill, on the ground that the section of the constitution quoted empowered the legislature to make general provisions for filling unexpired terms, not to make special provision for single cases.[4] The bill was passed over his veto.

Although Republican power was now doomed in a few weeks, and although resistance to a legislature which could easily override his vetoes was futile, yet Conley stubbornly continued to offer obstructions to the legislature at every possible point up to the very day when his successor was inaugurated.[5] He exhibited a courage and a political efficiency worthy of his predecessor, but accomplished nothing. He was able, however, to help his friends by means of the pardoning power. Several prominent Republicans were indicted at this time for various acts of public malfeasance. On the ground that in the existing state of public excitement these men could not obtain a fair trial, Conley ordered proceedings against several of these to be discontinued.[6]

On January 11, 1872, the returns from the special election

---

[1] Atlanta *Constitution*, Nov. 2, 1871.

[2] S. L., 1871, p. 27.   [3] Art. iv, sect. i, § 4.

[4] H. J., 1871, p. 179.

[5] For vetoed bills see S. L., 1871 and 1872, pp. 12, 15, 18, 27, 68, 74. See also *ibid.*, p. 260, and H. J., 1872, p. 25.

[6] E. M., 1870–74, p. 277 (pardon of V. A. Gaskill); Minutes of Fulton County Superior Court, vol. J, p. 404 (pardon of F. Blodgett).

were sent to the legislature by Conley, under protest,[1] and
James M. Smith was declared elected. On January 12,
Smith was inaugurated. Conley assisted at this ceremony,
thus yielding the last inch of Republican ground.[2]

Reviewing the events recorded from the beginning of this
chapter, we observe that the period of reconstruction in
Georgia was not a period when a swarm of harpies took possession of the state government and preyed at will upon a
helpless people. The constitutional convention of 1867–68
forebodes such a period, but when the Conservatives rouse
themselves, from that time on the stage presents an inter-
necine war between two very well matched enemies. This
struggle is usually represented as between a wicked assailant
and a righteous assailed. That it was a struggle between
Republicans and Democrats is much more characteristic.
In such a contest mutual vilifying of course abounded, and
it is not to be supposed *a priori* that the vilifying of one
party was more truthful than that of the other.

It is often vaguely said that reconstruction resulted in
government by carpet-baggers. John B. Gordon, the Conservative candidate for governor who was defeated by Bullock, expressed before a Congressional committee in 1870
the belief that there were not more than a dozen men holding offices in Georgia who had recently been non-residents.
He further said that the judges appointed by the Republican governor were entirely satisfactory.[3]

The reconstruction government is charged with having
imposed such heavy taxes that as a result the people were
impoverished, industry was checked, and many plantations
went to waste. During the decade before the war the law
provided that a tax should be annually levied at such a rate
as to produce $375,000, provided the rate should not exceed

[1] H. J., 1872, p. 25.   [2] *Ibid.*, p. 31.
[3] K. K. R., vol. 6, p. 327.

one-twelfth of one per cent.[1]   The revenue law of 1866 provided that a tax should be levied at such a rate as to produce $350,000.[2]   Owing to the vast destruction of property during the war, this necessitated a higher rate than that before the war.   The law of 1867 ordered a levy at such a rate as to raise $500,000.[3]   This law, made by the Johnson government, before reconstruction began, was continued by the legislature in the four following years.[4]   In 1870 the rate of assessment was two-fifths of one per cent.[5]   This rate was much higher than the one prevailing before the war, but this misfortune cannot be charged to reconstruction, since the reconstruction government merely followed the example of the Johnson government.

That the reconstruction *régime* did not do the economic harm often attributed to it is shown by the fact that during that *régime* the value of land and of all property in the state steadily increased, as appears from the following table:

	Land.	ASSESSED VALUATION. Town and City Property.	Total Property.
1868[6]	$79,727,584	$40,315,621	$191,235,520
1869[7]	84,577,166	44,368,096	204,481,706
1870[8]	95,600,674	47,922,544	226,119,519
1871[9]	96,857,512	52,159,734	234,492,468

Nevertheless, the reconstruction government spent the public money extravagantly.   This fact is shown by a comparison of the expenditures of the state under Bullock's administration and under that of his predecessor.   Such a comparison, it is true, has been employed to prove the contrary.   Governor Bullock was wont to rebut charges of extravagance by showing that the state spent more under Jenkins' administration than under his, in proportion to the

---

[1] Digest of tax laws, 1859, p. 11.   [2] S. L., 1865–66, p. 253.

[3] *Ibid.*, 1866, p. 164.   [4] *Ibid.*, 1868, p. 152; 1869, p. 159.

[5] B. L., p. 11.   [6] C. R., 1870 (printed in S. J., 1870, part ii, p. 83).

[7] C. R., 1870.   [8] C. R., April, 1871.   [9] C. R., April, 1872.

time occupied by each.[1]   This was true, as the following
figures show :[2]

Gross expenditures in 1866 and 1867 ....$3,223,323.46
Average annual expenditure during these years........ 1,601,661.73
Gross expenditures from August 11, 1868, to Jan. 1, 1870.. 2,260,252.15
Gross expenditures in 1870 .... 1,444,816.73
Gross expenditures in 1871 .... 1,476,978.86
Average annual expenditure during this period........ 1,554,614.32

A comparison of gross expenditures, however, is of no
significance unless the sums contrasted represent payments
for the same purposes.   Under the earlier administration the
government undertook large expeditures for the relief of
destitute persons, especially of wounded soldiers and the
relicts of soldiers.[3]   This accounts for the remarkable size of
the amounts credited to " special appropriations" in the
report for 1866 and 1867.   Under Bullock's administration
the government spent nothing for these purposes.   For a
fair comparison of the economy of the Johnson government
and the reconstruction government, it is necessary to com-
pare the amounts which they spent respectively for the same
objects.   Their payments for the more important adminis-
trative purposes are shown in the following table :[4]

	1866.	1867.	1868.	1869.	1870.	1871.
Civil Establishment.	$20,771.66	$75,222.44	$50,373.72	$85,666.41	$77,851.77	$78,365.21
Contingent Fund ...	6,128.62	15,430.74	10,059.06	19,968.16	38,284.44	20,296.95
Printing Fund ...	1,021.75	16,114.90	20,452.96	7,673.38	60,011.78	20,000.00
Special Appropriations ...	304,955.05	879,897.77	210,916.11	261,097.37	260,442.85	806,419.08

[1] B. L., p. 9; B. A., p. 42.

[2] Report of state treasurer Jones, published in H. J., 1868, p. 361; R. C., 1870;
R. C., April, 1871; R. C., April, 1872.

[3] S. L., 1865– 1866, pp. 12 and 14; *ibid.*,, 1866, pp. 10, 11, 143.

[4] Compiled from the financial documents above cited.

These figures show that almost all the annual expenditures of Bullock's administration, aside from " special appropriations," were well above those of the preceding administration, and that the payments from the printing fund, especially in 1870, and from the contingent fund in 1870, were so large as to convict the administration of great extravagance.

The reconstruction legislature was reproached because of its large *per diem*—nine dollars. This *per diem* was established by the Johnson government,[1] and is, therefore, not a charge against reconstruction. But the other expenses of the legislature fully corroborate the charges of extravagance made against it. This is shown by the following table :[2]

	Length of Session.	Total Expenditure.	Average Expenditure per month.
1865 and 1866.	Dec. 4 to Dec. 15. Jan. 15 to March 13. Nov. 1 to Dec. 14. ———— 3⅔ months.	$121,759.75	$33,207.18
1867.	No session.		
1868 and 1869.	July 4 to Oct. 6. Jan. 13 to March 18. ———— 5⁸⁄₁₆ months.	$446,055.00	$84,161.33
1870.	Jan. 10 to Feb. 17. Apr. 18 to May 4. July 6 to Oct. 25. ———— 5½ months.	$526,891.00	$95,798.32

[1] S. L., 1865–66, p. 250.

[2] Compiled from the financial reports above cited.

The enemies of reconstruction were fond of placing the state expenses of Bullock's administration in juxtaposition with those before the war. Contrasts truly

The state debt created by the reconstruction government was of two kinds; direct and contingent. When the reconstruction government went into operation the state debt was $6,544,500.[1] The reconstruction government incurred a bonded debt of $4,880,000.[2] This includes bonds to the

---

horrible could thus be produced. But it was not a fair comparison, for the expenses in such circumstances as prevailed after the war and after the social revolution would naturally be larger than before. The expenses of many states besides those which enjoyed reconstruction increased largely after the war. *E. g.* the records of Pennsylvania show that " Expenses of Government" were—

In 1857 .... $423,448.89
    1858 .... 399,888.36
    1860 .... 404,863.41
    1866 .... 668,909.63
    1867 .... 802,878.58
    1868 .... 845,539.89
    1869 .... 804,730.17
    1870 .... 826,069.25

Pennsylvania Executive Documents, Auditor's Reports, for the years named. In Massachusetts the "Ordinary Expenses" were—

In 1857 .... $1,236,204.26
    1858 .... 1,008,620.50
    1859 .... 999,899.76
    1860 .... 1,193,896.41
    1866 .... 6,877,720.85
    1867 .... 5,953,003.31
    1868 .... 5,908,678.48

Massachusetts Public Documents for the years named.

[1] C. R., 1870.

[2] C. R., April, 1871, p. 14; C. R., April, 1872, p. 17; B. L., p. 13; Conley's message to the legislature, Jan. 11, 1872 (quoted in B. A., p. 6, and in K. K. R., vol. i, p. 141).

Of these bonds 3,000, representing a debt of $3,000,000, were issued under a law of Sept. 15, 1870 (S. L., 1870, p. 10), authorizing the governor to issue bonds for various purposes without specified limit as to amount. The rest were issued under an act of Oct. 17, 1870 (omitted from the session laws, see Conley's message just cited), authorizing the governor to issue to the Brunswick and Albany railroad state bonds to the amount of $1,880,000 in exchange for bonds of the railroad to the amount of $2,350,000.

In addition to the bonds already mentioned, bonds to the amount of $600,000

amount of $1,880,000 which were issued to a railroad in exchange for its bonds to a greater amount and bearing interest at the same rate. This amount, therefore, was not a burden on the state, provided the railroad remained solvent; though in form a direct, it was virtually a contingent liability. Further, $300,000 of the money borrowed was used to pay the principal of the old debt. Deducting these two sums, we find that the burden of direct debt was increased by $2,700,000.

Contingent debt was incurred by the indorsement of railroad bonds. In 1868 the state offered aid of this kind to three railroad companies,[1] in 1869 to four,[2] and in 1870 to thirty.[3] The state offered to indorse the bonds of each of these companies to the amount, usually, of from $12,000 to $15,000 per mile, sometimes more and sometimes less. If all the roads had accepted the full amount of aid offered, the state would have become contingently liable for about $30,-

---

were issued under acts of 1868 (S. L., 1868, pp. 14 and 138.) These were not sold and were returned to the possession of the state during Bullock's administration (Angier's statement, K. K. R., vol. 6, p. 162). Also, before the issue of $3,000,000 mentioned, bonds to the amount of $2,000,000 were issued (Conley's message cited). These were hypothecated with several bankers in New York. Some of them, amounting to $500,000, were returned and cancelled during Bullock's administration (Conley's message). The rest, amounting to $1,500,000, remained in the hands of the bankers. Conley stated, in January, 1872 (message cited), that these bonds had been replaced by bonds of a later issue and canceled during Bullock's administration, and had therefore ceased to be a claim against the state. This statement conflicts with three facts. 1. The bankers who held these bonds refused to return them after their alleged cancellation. 2. One of these bankers sold the bonds which he held after their alleged cancellation (Henry Clews, *Twenty-eight Years in Wall Street*, p. 277). 3. The legislature of Georgia repudiated these bonds in 1872, which would have been unnecessary if they had been cancelled. It seems probable, therefore, though not certain, that this $1,500,000 should be added to the debt incurred by the reconstruction government.

[1] S. L., 1868, title xvii.   [2] *Ibid.*, 1869, title xv.

[3] *Ibid.*, 1870, title xi, division vii.

000,000.[1] But only six roads accepted, and the contingent
liability thus created was $6,923,400.[2] The laws offering the
aid involved little risk to the state; they made substantial
progress in construction and substantial evidence of sound-
ness conditions precedent to indorsement, and secured to
the state a lien on all the property of each road in case it
defaulted. The indorsement of railroad bonds is not a re-
proach to the reconstruction government. The great policy
of that government, when it was sufficiently free from partisan labors to have a policy, was to repair the prosperity of
the state, and the construction of railroads was an important
means to this end.[3]

The worst stain on the reconstruction government is its
management of the state railroad. The Western and At-
lantic Railroad, owned and operated by the state until 1871,
was placed under the superintendence of Foster Blodgett by
the governor in January, 1870.[4] Thenceforth hundreds of
employees were discharged to make room for Republican
favorites; important positions were filled by strangers to
the business; the receipts were stolen,[5] or squandered in
purchases made from other Republicans at monstrous prices;
and the road suffered great dilapidation.[6]

The preferred object of the Conservative abuse in the re-

---

[1] Angier's statement, K. K. R., vol. i, p. 129.

[2] Conley's message above cited.

[3] It is to be remarked, however, that four of the roads whose bonds the state
had guaranteed became bankrupt before 1874. See Poor's Railroad Manual for
1873-4, pp. 432 and 582; and for 1874-5, p. 426.

[4] E. M., 1870-74, p. 449.

[5] See the case of Hoyt, Minutes of Fulton County Superior Court, vol. I, pp.
371, 445.

[6] Report of the investigating committee of the legislature appointed in Dec.,
1871. Its report was printed in Atlanta in 1872. It is bitterly partisan, but a
minority report made by a Republican admits, with humorous resignation, that
the charges are true.

construction government was Governor Bullock. We have
seen that he was remarkably powerful as well as remarkably
active in promoting the interests of his party. He was
abused for that. For the extravagance of the state government the governor was held largely responsible. He was
abused for that. But he was further accused of fraud in
financial matters.

Although this charge has never been established, the
public had some excuse for believing it at the time. As a
result of the quarrel between the governor and the treasurer,
the governor ordered the bankers who were the financial
agents of the state to hold no further communication with
the treasurer after June 3, 1869, but to communicate only
with the governor.[1] The effect upon the public was an impression of great confusion and irregularity in the finances
The treasurer's reports could not give a complete account of
state moneys, and the governor was not careful to inform
the public of the condition of that part of the finances over
which he had assumed control. Moreover, the governor and
the treasurer kept up a constant iuterchange of accusation
and insinuation in the newspapers. In another way the
governor put himself in an unfortunate light. In his letter
to the Ku Klux Committee his statements regarding his bond
transactions were so vague as to give the impression (rightly
or wrongly) of a desire to conceal something.[2] The same
laxity of statement appears in Conley's statement of the use to
which the bonds issued by Bullock had been put.[3] His sudden resignation and departure on the eve of a threatened
investigation seemed to confirm the evidence of his guilt.

But though he did not keep the public informed, it has

[1] A. A. C., 1869, p. 305.
[2] See K. K. R., vol. i, pp. 137 and 138. The statements are on pp. 11 and 12
of the letter as published in Atlanta in 1871.
[3] See Conley's message cited.

never been established that his accounts were wrong. He
spent money freely, and in some cases without authority;[1]
but none of his accusers has ever proved that he spent any
without regular and correct record by the comptroller. And
though he issued bonds perhaps in excess, he issued none
without proper registration in the comptroller's records.[2]
His apparent efforts to conceal facts do not prove fraud; a
sufficient motive would be furnished by desire to conceal
the extravagance of his administration. Furthermore, he has
been positively acquitted of the charge of fraud. In 1878
he returned to Georgia, and the courts proceeded to give
him " a speedy and public trial."   Of his many alleged
crimes, indictments were secured for three.   One indictment
was quashed,[3] Upon the other two the verdict was " not
guilty."[4]   His resignation was explained in a letter to his
" political friends," published on October 31, 1871.[5]   He said
that he had obtained evidence of a concerted design among

---

[1] In the latter part of 1868 and in 1869 the governor paid to a certain H. I.
Kimball $54,500 from the treasury. He paid this to be used in furnishing a
building which was at that time occupied as the state capital. (Bullock's statement, B. A., p. 29.) There was no law authorizing this payment, nor was the
state under any obligation to make it. The state bought the building in 1870 by
an act of the legislature which provided that the $54,500 should be counted as
part of the price. Thus Bullock's advance was ratified by the state. (S. L.,
1870, p. 494.) This, however, does not change the character of the act.

[2] See C. R., April, 1871, and April, 1872. Bullock was accused of indorsing
the bonds of three railroads contrary to law. In the case of two of these (the
Cartersville and Van Wert, or Cherokee railroad, and the Bainbridge, Cuthbert
and Columbus railroad) he refuted the charge beyond contradiction in his
address to the public of 1872. In the case of the third (the Brunswick and
Albany railroad) he admitted that he had indorsed bonds before the road had
complied with the conditions required by law, but said that he did it for the public
good. (B. A., pp. 39-41.)

[3] Atlanta *Constitution*, Jan. 3, 1878; Minutes of the Fulton County Superior
Court, vol. N, p. 261.

[4] *Ibid.*, pp. 263, 273.

[5] Atlanta *New Era*, Oct. 31, 1871. Printed as an appendix to B. A.

certain prominent members of the incoming legislature to impeach him (as they could easily do, with the immense Conservative majority), and instal as governor the Conservative who would be elected president of the senate. To resign and put the governorship in the hands of a Republican who could not be impeached was the only way to defeat this " nefarious scheme." This explanation was of course ignored by Bullock's enemies when it was made; but in view of the lack of evidence that he was guilty of any fraud, and in view of the positive evidence to the contrary, there is now no reason to doubt it.

The governor made extraordinary use of the pardoning power. According to a statement sanctioned by him, he pardoned four hundred and ninety-eight criminals, forty-one of whom were convicted or accused of murder, fifty-two of burglary, five of arson, and eight of robbery.[1] The leader of the Conservative party at that time, B. H. Hill, emphatically declared in a public statement that the governor had no worse motive than " kindness of heart." [2]

To sum up the case against the reconstruction government, we have seen that it was extravagant, that it mismanaged the state railroad, and that it pardoned a great many criminals. It was not guilty of the enormities often associated with reconstruction; but it was a government composed of men who obtained polictical position only through the interference of an outside power—it was the product of a system conceived partly in vengeance, partly in folly, and partly in political strategy, and imposed by force. It was hated partly for what it did, but more for what it was.

[1] Appendix to B. L. (printed in K. K. R., vol. 7, p. 825).
[2] K. K. R., vol. 7, pp. 767 and 780.

CHAPTER X

CONCLUSION

A CONFEDERATE veteran recently remarked amid great applause at an assembly in Atlanta that there never was a conqueror so magnanimous as the North, for within six years from the surrender of the southern armies she had allowed the South to take part in her national councils. Nevertheless, within those six years the Congressional Disciplinarians gave the South a discipline which she will never forget. It did not result in permanent estrangement between the North and the South, for sectional bitterness seems extinct. But whether there was any profit in it—whether, in case the South never again attempts to secede, that happy omission will be due to reconstruction—may be doubted.

Was there a clearer gain from the humanitarian point of view? We have seen that at the close of the war a spirit of gratitude and philanthropy prevailed among the most influential of the southern white people as regards the negroes. Instead of allowing this spirit to develop and in the course of time to produce its natural results, the North, believing that suffrage was essential to the negro's welfare and progress, forced the South to enfranchise him, by reconstruction. This caused the negro untold immediate harm (since reconstruction was a contributary cause of Kukluxism), and delayed his ultimate advance by giving the friendly spirit of the white people a check in its development from which it has not yet recovered.

From the point of view of the Republican Politicians, reconstruction at first succeeded, but later proved a mistaken policy. By it they lost the support of the southern white men who had been opposed to secession. These formed a large party in Georgia. The victory of the federal arms had the nature of a party victory for them. They would have added their strength to the Republican party. Reconstruction, with its threat of negro domination, drove them into the Democratic party, where they still remain. For a time this loss was made good by negro votes, but not long.

Without reconstruction there would have been no Fifteenth Amendment. But the good will and philanthropy of the people among whom the negro lives, which reconstruction took away, would have brought him more benefit than the Fifteenth Amendment. Without reconstruction there would have been no Fourteenth Amendment. But a long line of decisions of the Supreme Court has determined that the Fourteenth Amendment did not achieve the nationalization of civil rights—an end which might justify reconstruction as a means. In short, reconstruction seems to have produced bad government, political rancor, and social violence and disorder, without compensating good.

BIBLIOGRAPHY.

PUBLIC RECORDS AND DOCUMENTS.

Of the United States Government.

Congressional Globe.

Public Documents.

Statutes at Large.

Supreme Court Reports.

Military orders in the archives of the Department of War.

Correspondence in the same archives.

Correspondence in the archives of the Department of State.

Unpublished records in the same archives.

Of the Government of Georgia.

Journal of the constitutional convention of 1865.

Journal of the constitutional convention of 1867–8.

Journals of the legislature.

Reports of the four committees appointed by the legislature in December, 1871 to investigate respectively—

The management of the state railroad.

The lease of the same road.

The official conduct of Governor Bullock.

The transactions of Governor Bullock's administration relating to the issue of state bonds and the indorsement of railroad bonds.

These reports were published in Atlanta in 1872.

Session Laws.

Supreme Court Reports.

Reports of the State Comptroller.

Executive minutes in the archives of the state in Atlanta.

Minutes of the Fulton County Superior Court in the office of that court in Atlanta.

NEWSPAPERS.

Atlanta *New Era.*

Atlanta *Constitution.*

Milledgeville *Federal Union* (during the war called the *Confederate Union*).

Savannah *News.*

Savannah *Republican.*

CONTEMPORARY PAMPHLETS.

A letter from Rufus B. Bullock to the chairman of the Ku Klux committee, Atlanta, 1871.

Address of the same to the people of Georgia, dated October, 1872.

Letter from the same "to the Republican Senators and Representatives who support the Reconstruction Acts," Washington, May 21, 1870.

HISTORICAL WORKS AND COMPENDIA.

American Annual Cyclopædia. New York.

Avery, I. W., *History of Georgia.* New York, 1881.

Bancroft, F. A., *The Negro in Politics.* New York, 1885.

Clews, Henry, *Twenty-eight Years in Wall Street.* London, 1888.

Cox, S. S., *Three Decades of Federal Legislation.* Providence, 1886.

Dunning, W. A., *The Civil War and Reconstruction.* New York, 1898.

Fielder, H., *The Life and Times of Joseph E. Brown.* Springfield, Mass., 1883.

Hill, B. H., Jr., *The Life, Speeches and Writings of Benjamin H. Hill.* Atlanta, 1891.

Lalor, J. J., *Cyclopædia of Political Science.* New York, 1893. Articles on Reconstruction, Georgia, and Ku Klux.

Poor, H. V., *Manual of the Railroads of the United States.* New York, publishe yearly.

Sherman, W. T., *Memoirs.* New York, 1875.

Stephens, Alex., *The War between the States.* Philadelphia, 1868–70.

Taylor, Richard, *Destruction and Reconstruction.* New York, 1893.

Tribune Almanac. New York.

Wilson, Henry, *History of the Reconstruction Measures.* Hartford, 1868.